"How to" guide

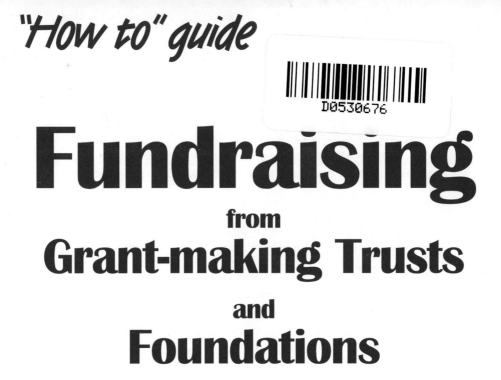

D0530676

Fundraising

from
Grant-making Trusts
and
Foundations

Karen Gilchrist
Margo Horsley

DIRECTORY OF SOCIAL CHANGE

Published by
The Directory of Social Change
24 Stephenson Way
London NW1 2DP
Tel: 020 7209 5151, fax: 020 7209 5049
e-mail: info@dsc.org.uk
from whom further copies and a full publications list are available

The Directory of Social Change is a Registered Charity no. 800517

ISBN 1 900360 77 2

British Library Cataloguing in Publication Data
A catalogue record for this book is available from the British Library

Cover design by Lenn Darroux
Text designed by Sarah Nicholson
Typeset, printed and bound by Stephen Austin, Hertford

Other Directory of Social Change departments in London:
Courses and Conferences tel: 020 7209 4949
Charity Centre tel: 020 7209 1015
Research tel: 020 7209 4422
Finance and Administration tel: 020 7209 0902

Directory of Social Change Northern Office:
Federation House, Hope Street, Liverpool L1 9BW
Courses and Conferences tel: 0151 708 0117
Research tel: 0151 708 0136

Contents

About the authors

Karen Gilchrist is a researcher and writer. She is the director of the media and communications company Resource Base, which works in social, educational and cultural affairs. Karen was previously a journalist with the magazines *Marketing Week* and *Televisual* before working in television as a social action researcher. She has also been a cross-media coordinator with the charity Community Service Volunteers and worked for TVS Education and Community before helping to set up Resource Base.

Margo Horsley works independently as an adviser to and trainer for trusts, foundations, Lottery distributors and charities. She was part of the first-phase team that set up the National Lottery Charities Board in 1995, and was subsequently involved in grant-programme development at both Sport England and the New Opportunities Fund. Since 1991 Margo has been executive director, part time, of the Meridian Broadcasting Charitable Trust. She is also a member of the Institute of Fundraising Managers and chaired the conference 2000 planning group for the Association of Charitable Foundations.

Introduction

Grant-making trusts and foundations are set up to give money to charitable activities so that they can achieve a particular purpose ... and you want to raise money for your good cause. The challenge is to show how your project can help a trust, or trusts, to achieve their purpose; and to put your case for funding as effectively as possible.

This guide aims to help you do just that.

Who is this guide for?

It is designed to help people who are raising money for their voluntary, community or charitable organisation, and who may be relatively new to fundraising from grant-making trusts and foundations. Advice on raising money for individuals is not given here.

Trusts and foundations account for a large proportion of charitable giving in the UK. So it's an area no fundraiser can really afford to ignore.

Trusts' and foundations' support

There are almost 9,000 grant-making trusts and foundations in the UK, giving around £1.25 billion each year. And you can add to this the £320 million given by the National Lottery Charities Board, and the £300 million from charities such as Imperial Cancer Research and Oxfam, who give grants in the course of their work. That makes donations of around £1.9 billion per year in total.

As a comparison, voluntary and charitable organisations receive more funds from trusts than they do from companies, while funding from central or local government (excluding grants to housing associations and employment schemes) is at an equivalent level.

Research by the Charities Aid Foundation (see *Dimensions 2000* volume 3) revealed that about a third of all grants are made in the area of social care, accounting for a quarter of the amount of money provided by trusts. Education, the arts and health also received significant sums of money from trusts.

Trusts or foundations

Throughout this book we are going to talk about 'trusts' to refer to both trusts and foundations. The terms are virtually interchangeable. All charitable foundations are trusts (that is they are managed by trustees). A foundation is a trust whose income comes from an endowment of land or invested capital. Not all foundations make grants, however. Some fund charitable work of their own.

Guidelines but not a formula

There are no magic formulae that will guarantee success when you are fundraising from grant-making trusts. But there are some basic guidelines that should help. Some are quite obvious; others become clearer after you have made several trust applications – particularly if you receive feedback from the trusts concerned.

This book might save you some of the frustration involved in being turned down because you have approached the wrong trust at the wrong time; asked for an inappropriate sum of money for the wrong piece of work; or failed to present your project and organisation effectively. And it might help you to celebrate a successful application to the right trust, at the right time, for the right sum of money, and for the right project – a project that helps the trust to achieve its purpose.

What is in this 'How To' guide?

In this guide we start with the wider picture – providing an overview of grant-making trusts, looking at what motivates them, what they are trying to achieve and what they will and won't fund. Then we look at how you can put together your case for support, find the appropriate trusts to approach and make your application. We talk about how your proposal will be assessed, And then we look forward to how you might work together with your trust funders, following the sequence set out below.

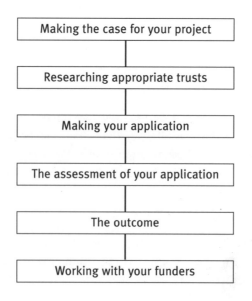

Making the case for your project

Researching appropriate trusts

Making your application

The assessment of your application

The outcome

Working with your funders

Grant-making trusts – what are they?

In the first two chapters we provide some background information on grant-making trusts – outlining the different types of trusts and foundations, and exploring the reasons why they give their money to charities, voluntary organisations and community groups. It is important to understand their perspective. If you can appreciate what they are looking for and what they are trying to achieve, then this will help you approach the right trusts with appropriate proposals.

Making the case for your project

Before you can think about approaching a grant-making trust you need to be clear about what it is you are asking for. You need a clear and strong case for your project, or piece of work.

We take you through this process in Chapter 3. As a result you will have come up with a project plan. This will form the basis of your application to potential trust funders.

You might need to emphasise different elements of your project proposal to different trusts. And you might need to extract some information to include in an application form. The original plan, or 'case', though, remains a good starting point. It is also useful later on, when you want to evaluate the success of your project.

Only once you have put together the case for your project will you be able to carry out research into the various trusts you should approach.

Researching and approaching appropriate trusts

Who will you approach? In Chapter 4 we look at the importance of researching different trusts. And we discuss some of the support available – from reference books and CD-ROMs, as well as advice organisations.

Different trusts have different approaches and attitudes to providing information about their grant making. Some trusts provide guidelines on what they will and won't fund. A small number issue application forms to ensure the applicant gives all the information required. Others provide less detail. Some will discuss your project on the phone to help determine whether you should apply or not.

So, you need to be prepared to spend quite a bit of time and effort finding out about trusts that are interested in the sort of work you are proposing.

Armed with as much detailed information as possible on various trusts, you will be able to put together a hit-list of appropriate ones. And once you have done this, you will be ready to approach them.

Making your application

In Chapter 5 we consider your written application for funding. We look at how you can adapt the case so that you present it in the most appropriate way. We look at some of the techniques that can help you present your project effectively, thereby improving your chances of success. We also discuss application forms – used by a few of the larger grant-making trusts.

The assessment of your application

Once you have submitted your application, what happens to it? How do the trusts decide what to fund? It can be helpful to know who is likely to read your proposal and what they will do with it. We also ask: 'How will you prepare yourselves if the trust asks to visit?' We cover this in Chapter 6.

Working with a trust

Chapter 7 looks at what happens once a trust has agreed to support your work. It is useful to know this before you start so that you are prepared to build a good on-going relationship with them.

Further information

Finally, we outline further sources of information and advice, while our appendix contains useful details of some of the largest grant-making trusts in the UK.

Grant-making trusts – what are they? Part one: their origins

In this chapter you will find background information on:

▶ Grant-making trusts (what they are and how they are set up)

▶ The way different trusts come into being, and where their money comes from

▶ How the origins of a trust can affect the way it continues to operate

▶ Some of the other grant makers you might consider that are not covered by this book

Your work can help certain trusts to achieve their goals, so you need to know why they exist and what motivates them. They have money to distribute and a purpose to fulfil. You have the ability to turn their broad goals into local action through your work.

Some basic background

- **Trusts are charitable organisations** – all grant-making trusts are charities. And those based in England and Wales are registered with the Charity Commission, like other charities of their size. A grant-making trust can make tax-free donations. It doesn't pay tax on its income.

- **A trust is founded by a 'settlor'** – a trust or foundation is usually established by a 'settlor' (an individual or organisation) who allocates it some money, property or shares. The settlor and the trustees decide on the aims of the trust and its charitable purpose. This is outlined in a trust deed which also gives details of the trust's original assets and trustees.

- **Trusts come in a variety of shapes and sizes** – some are large national, or even international, grant makers; the vast majority are relatively small. Of the 8,800 or so trusts in the UK, only the top 300 employ full-time staff. The rest rely on part time or voluntary administrators, or are handled by firms of lawyers or accountants.
- **Trustees take grant-making decisions** – some trusts employ administrators who make phone calls, visit applicants and carry out detailed interviews. But the ultimate decision on the allocation of any grant remains with the trustees. It is the trustees who are responsible for running the trust and making grants.

Trusts have different roots

Trusts have different origins. Some are established by individuals, others by organisations. The main distinctions are between:

- family trusts;
- company trusts;
- trusts that need to raise money each year;
- community trusts and foundations;
- the National Lottery Charities Board (which isn't strictly speaking a 'trust', as we shall see below).

Let's look in more detail at these different types of trust now.

Family trusts

If an individual or organisation wants to donate a lot of money, then there are ways to give tax-effectively – through Gift Aid, for instance. However, if you have to fill out the appropriate forms for each gift this can be time-consuming and quite bureaucratic. It's much more straightforward to hand over a lump sum to a grant-making trust, and do the paperwork once a year (or even once in a lifetime).

A number of grant-making trusts are set up to distribute money left by a person in their Will. For whatever reason, the individual decides to leave their accumulated wealth to others through a grant-making trust.

There is quite a history of wealthy people giving some of their money to support charitable work in this way – stretching back to Victorian times. Over 150 of the trusts in existence today were set up before 1900.

Frequently it is the people who have acquired wealth in their lifetimes who establish trusts. A number of people who have been successful in business, along with actors, entertainers, musicians, sports stars, artists – even lottery winners – have set up trusts.

Those who have inherited their money also set up trusts. But often there is already a family grant-making trust in existence.

Wealthy people set up trusts for many different reasons, including because they:

- can afford to;
- want to use their wealth to help others (particularly in their field of expertise);
- believe in and support a particular cause;
- feel guilty about their success;
- have had a personal experience of illness, disadvantage or something similar.

Such trusts won't always be established with a gift of money. They might be endowed with stocks and shares, or with property.

Small family trusts

Many of the smaller trusts remain closely connected with the person who made the initial donation (the settlor) and their family. The small family trusts might be left money during someone's lifetime or in their memory.

Some of these family trusts are administered by accountants or solicitors. And some can be quite inactive, or 'dormant'. Many of the smaller trusts have very little money to distribute.

Small family trusts tend not to encourage applications because of the administration involved and the lack of funds available. So it is not unusual to send off an application to a small trust and receive no reply.

You might strike lucky with a small family trust – either by being one of a handful of causes receiving regular support, or by discovering a dormant trust and successfully applying for funding. However, they are unlikely to have huge sums of money at their disposal, so you have to balance the effort you make to find them with the time you put into applications to the larger trusts.

A small charity was trying to raise money to fund the repairs of an ancient church building. The fundraiser was proud to have found two small family trusts that hadn't paid out any money for years. She approached them successfully, receiving £700 from each for the building fund. It had taken about five solid days of research to find these hidden family trusts. It's hard to compare this effort with the many additional weeks spent identifying large trusts and preparing applications, responding to their enquiries and so on. But it's worth noting that the fund received £80,000 from six other, well-publicised trusts.

Company trusts

Many companies give sums of money to charity each year. This might be because they:

- see themselves as playing an important role in the local community;
- want to be seen to be responsible;
- are trying to generate goodwill;
- would like a 'good' reputation;
- want their staff to feel good about their organisation.

Company donations can be made in a variety of ways. If the amounts are small and infrequent the company will often just write out a cheque. If the amounts are larger the company might make its payments through the Charities Aid Foundation. Or it might set up a company grant-making trust.

There are tax advantages for companies who make their charitable donations through a trust. Instead of having to complete the paperwork for every gift, the company has to do this just once a year, or every time it makes a donation to its associated trust.

Many company trusts are not truly independent of their parent. And that means that decisions on funding might be influenced by public relations and marketing considerations. It's important to know this when you approach such a trust for support, because your request would need to be more like a sponsorship proposal. You would need to emphasise the branding benefits for the company and the close association between the company's target audience and the people you will reach. This type of trust is listed in *The Guide to UK Company Giving*.

Independent of the founding company

There are some large foundations that have been set up by companies and that are considered to be independent grant makers. These trusts are listed in *A Guide to the Major Trusts* volumes 1–3.

Once they have been set up these independent trusts have their own resources. And they continually use their investments to generate income. The original trust deed will probably mean that a trust gives its grants in an area possessing at least a loose connection with the work of the company that set it up – perhaps giving grants in the general field of medical research if the money originally came from a pharmaceutical company, for instance. But the trust will be based in a different building, with its own staff, and have trustees with little or no connection to the company.

A trust which was originally established by a healthcare company is now completely independent. However, it still focuses its grant making in the area of health, ageing and disability, which reflects its founding company's intentions. Another was set up by a financial services company. It provides support to community regeneration projects, and work aimed at tackling poverty in urban and rural areas. Again these funding priorities stem from the area of the business of the founding organisation. But the trust makes its decisions completely independently of company employees or shareholders.

Staff trusts

Another type of company trust is set up by the staff themselves. The staff raise funds, perhaps through the profits from an employee lottery scheme. They then distribute the funds through their trust. Many such schemes give grants to charities nominated by staff who have some close connection with them. But others are willing to consider applications from all local community groups.

Two pre-school playgroups, working with families in an area of high unemployment, wrote to a local company trust asking for similar sums of money for new books, toys and equipment. The requests were considered at the same quarterly trustees' meeting. One of the playgroups had an employee of the company on its management committee – it received £500. The other had no links with the company – it received nothing.

Religious and international foundations

There are a number of grant-making trusts which have been set up to promote a particular faith. Some are set up by a particular faith community, others by religious and successful individuals.

Some grant-making trusts in this country may be set up as branches of international foundations. The Calouste Gulbenkian Foundation is an example of an international foundation with an arm in the UK.

Sources of income

The trusts that we have considered so far have a guaranteed regular income, from:

- further donations from the founding company, or individual 'settlor';
- land or property;
- interest earned on shares or cash.

Some, however, have to raise money before they can give it away. And they raise this money from a variety of sources.

Fundraising grant makers

Fundraising grant makers come in a variety of shapes and sizes.

Major fundraising grant makers

There are some major grant makers who are dependent on successful fundraising campaigns. Broadcast appeals such as Comic Relief and BBC Children in Need are examples. Imperial Cancer Research and some of the other charities that give grants in the course of their work also rely on fundraising. They raise their money from a variety of sources – the usual fundraising mix of individuals, companies, trusts, lottery distributors and so on.

The large fundraising grant makers are very active in supporting a wide range of different charitable initiatives.

Smaller fundraising grant makers

There are other smaller fundraising grant makers set up to raise money for specific local organisations – such as hospitals, schools and universities. These include PTAs (parent teacher associations), and 'friends of' groups. Some families set up fundraising appeals on behalf of their children, or in their memory. These organisations are focused on their particular cause and are unlikely to consider approaches from other charities.

Community trusts and foundations

Community trusts are set up by groups of local people or organisations to raise money and distribute funds for the local community. The aim is to meet the needs of local people through local resources.

The Community Foundations Network describes community trusts as: 'active fundraising and grant-making organisations committed to building permanent endowment and working within defined geographic areas'.

Some community trusts receive regular income from land or property, others have to fundraise. But whatever their financial set-up, they are established to tackle local need.

Some community trusts are quite involved in conducting research into local need, as well as funding local groups.

Community trusts are often very active, highly publicised and ready to back innovative and emerging organisations. To find out if there is a community trust in your area, contact the Community Foundations Network (see *Further information* for contact details).

A self-help group established by a group of young carers met once a week for a mix of social activities and to provide support to one another. The young people were concerned that some young carers couldn't play a full part in the group because of the cost of some of the leisure activities. The local community foundation provided them with a grant to cover the cost of outings, and also helped put the group in touch with a local community facility, which they might use as a base. The young carers' group and the community hall went on to apply successfully to a major trust to develop a community café – run and used by young carers and other 'young people at risk'.

A community foundation set up a three-year project to involve older people in the development of the county health and social welfare policy. This resulted in new solutions to existing problems as well as a greater understanding of the formation of policy and the constraints affecting practice.

Local authorities

Some local authorities administer trusts, created when an individual leaves them responsible for a sum of money left in their Will. There is often a quite general instruction about 'improving the local community' or 'supporting local young people'. The sums involved can be quite small – in fact too small for the council to bother with. So, again, such trusts can be inactive and hidden. Some local authority trusts, however, might be highly publicised grant-making 'community chests'.

To find out about these trusts it's worth getting in touch with either the council's chief executive's office, a grants officer or an external funding officer.

Trust 'lookalike' – the National Lottery Charities Board

The National Lottery Charities Board is not, strictly speaking, a trust, as it was set up by, and is answerable to, government. However, it is a member of the Association of Charitable Foundations (ACF), giving millions of pounds in grants to charities and community groups throughout the UK. In fact, in its first four years it gave over 18,000 grants worth more than a billion pounds.

An evolving grant maker

When the Charities Board began its grant making it was overwhelmed with applications. The number of applications far exceeded funds – and only one in six was successful. At the time of writing, the success rate for applicants is more like one in two.

Other things have changed since the Charities Board gave its first grants. Initially all the grant programmes had fixed deadlines and focused on themes such as young people or low income. These fixed deadlines meant that there was a closing date for applications, and all forms had to be submitted by this time if the application was to be considered. At that point the applications were reviewed by independent grant assessors.

The Charities Board has now introduced two 'rolling programmes' of grants:

- community involvement;
- poverty and disadvantage.

These have no fixed deadlines. There are still some programmes with such deadlines, however – with themes such as 'international grants' and 'health and social research'.

Grant assessors are now employed directly by the Charities Board; their reports are considered by an independent Regional Awards Committee. Usefully, the Board now provides feedback to unsuccessful applicants.

Some of the most common reasons for being turned down include:

- ineligibility to apply (if the organisation doesn't have an appropriate constitution or management committee, for example);
- the project falling outside the funding criteria;
- an incomplete application;
- an unrealistic or unachievable project.

The National Lottery Charities Board has a comprehensive website listing details of all its grants programmes, along with a database of groups that have received funding. It also publishes its grant assessment manual on the web (see *Further information* for contact details). This manual includes information on the general approach taken to 'scoring' applications, along with some of the specific criteria that are considered. An edited version also appears in the *Guide to the National Lottery Charities Board*.

Small grants from the Charities Board

Until June 2000 the Charities Board administered a programme of small grants known as 'Millennium Festival Awards for All'. This programme provided grants of between £500 and £5,000. A joint programme between various lottery distributors with one common simplified application form, it is set to continue after June 2000 as Awards for All.

> A group which provides support and accommodation to young people who are homeless received a small grant from the National Lottery Charities Board (through Awards for All). The grant helped pay for some new computer equipment and a series of publicity leaflets. The group had not previously applied to the Charities Board because it didn't want to ask for a large sum of money, and it had been put off by what it considered to be a lengthy application form.

Small grants are available for a wide range of projects. Priority is given to groups with an annual income of less than £15,000. If you are successful, the money is paid directly into your bank account – saving on time and administration.

Other grant makers

There are a number of other sources of funding for your work, including other grant makers. These include public bodies such as the Arts Council and Regional Arts Boards, Sport England, the New Opportunities Fund, local authorities, government departments and quangos (quasi-autonomous, non-governmental organisations).

Such non-trust grant makers are not the focus of this guide. However, many of the guidelines below might help you when you approach them for funding.

Grant-making trusts – what are they? Part two: their work

In this chapter you will discover:

▶ How trusts are managed
▶ What kinds of work trusts support
▶ How trusts reach decisions on what to fund
▶ The different types of funding trusts might provide
▶ The need to demonstrate your own sound financial management when making an application
▶ What kinds of work trusts do not fund

Some common characteristics

In the previous chapter we concentrated on some of the different ways trusts come into being. They are also set up and run in various different ways. The personalities of the founder or trustees can make a tremendous difference to the trust's approach to grant making. Many trusts sign up to guidelines on good practice drawn up by their umbrella body, the Association of Charitable Foundations, and all must comply with the law. There are some general observations that can be made about the way some trusts seem to share common aims to:

• create change;
• promote a better quality of life for those at greatest disadvantage;
• realise the potential of individuals and communities.

They may be interested in funding:

• new methods of tackling problems;
• projects which benefit disadvantaged and minority groups who have difficulty using traditional services, or who are inadequately provided for;

- responses to new, or newly found, problems or needs;
- projects which would be hard to fund through other fundraising methods;
- one-off projects, where this is not establishing a need for future funds even though there will be a long-term benefit (e.g. research);
- short and medium-term work which might attract funding from elsewhere, and which will have long-term benefit;
- in exceptional circumstances, core-funding for particular organisations – core-funding means support for the essential running costs of the organisation, the minimum resources needed to help the organisation to achieve its goals.

Many trusts pride themselves on being able to react to local need, by providing much-needed grants for projects which would come well down the list of any strategic agenda. In other words, they may be willing to consider small-scale projects that make a large diference to a limited number of people, rather than high-profile initiatives that reach hundreds or thousands of people. To some degree they could be said to have led the present government towards the provision of individual-centred services and facilities – those which focus on the individual (the user) rather than the service or facility itself.

The role of trustees

Trustees are totally responsible for the trust – for the way it is run and for the grants it gives. They take all decisions on policy, strategy and funding. Some trustees act as assessors, making visits to projects before reaching their decisions.

Administrators can help to gather information on a particular application and can add comments or a formal report. They can write letters, represent the trust at meetings and carry out research for the organisation, but they cannot award grants.

Trustees are duty bound to make decisions in accordance with the trust's purpose and policies.

Some trustees take a very dim view of being lobbied by grant applicants, so think very carefully before going down this route.

Working in many fields

Whilst there are some broad goals and approaches that many trusts share, they work in a range of different fields.

Their focus might be on one or more of the following broad areas, as defined in *Dimensions 2000* volume 3:

- education;
- health;
- social care;
- development and housing;
- arts, culture and recreations;
- religious activities;
- environment and animals;
- civil society, law and advocacy;
- international;
- science and technology;
- social science;
- philanthropy/volunteering.

Achieving their purpose

Trusts have a purpose they want to achieve in their particular field, or fields, of work. They can only achieve their purpose by:

- working through (supporting) many and different charitable organisations;
- ensuring that their support brings them into direct contact with communities;
- funding work at a local level;
- giving money to provide the resources necessary to carry out project work;
- funding work which they expect to fulfil their purpose and have long-lasting benefits.

But the funding is not for those things in themselves, it is to achieve their overall purpose.

A small educational group was set up to encourage teachers, and others working with young people, to value arts and creativity as a tool for learning. A major trust has identified arts and education as key areas for funding. One particular approach it wants to support is the establishment by teachers of self-help groups. The educational group promoting creativity was able to show the match between the purpose of the trust and its own work – and successfully applied for a grant. From the trust's perspective, it was able partly to achieve one of its purposes through the funding of the project.

More applications than funds

Even with 8,800 trusts and £1.9 billion of funding, there isn't enough money to go round. Trusts will almost always individually and collectively receive more applications than they can possibly fund.

So, they need to make decisions about what to fund and what not to fund.

A trust might have 'criteria', 'policies' or 'priorities' to help trustees reach these decisions. Some have quite a highly developed decision-making framework. And some publicise this framework as guidelines for those seeking grants.

Guidelines can help you to work out whether or not your project is the sort of thing that a particular trust would fund – you can 'self select' or 'self reject'. This can save you the time and effort of applying to inappropriate trusts. At the same time it cuts down on the amount a trust needs to spend on the administration of handling inappropriate applications.

Reaching decisions – a framework

The decision-making framework used by a trust might include some or all of the following elements:

- type of problem (or need) that has been identified and the applicant's proposed solution;
- type of activities the trust is willing to support;
- approaches used;
- types of funding;
- eligible organisations;
- area of geographical benefit;
- size of grant;
- funding period;
- financial and management capability.

Let's look at these elements in a bit more detail.

Solving problems/meeting needs

A trust might be especially interested in one or more particular problem or need.

The problem or need might be stated in general terms, such as 'rural poverty', or it might be linked with a particular target group – for instance: 'the poverty and disadvantage affecting unemployed people and their families in rural areas'.

Target groups might be communities of people linked by common need or disadvantage – such as young people, older people, carers, disabled people, or people from minority ethnic communities. They might be defined by the area in which they live; their need is taken as read.

Sometimes the way a trust states its target groups implies the area of need it is addressing. For instance, a trust might say that it supports work with 'young people at risk of offending', 'young people who have been excluded from school', and 'young unemployed people'. You might reasonably infer from this that the trust wants to address problems faced by socially excluded young people.

The important point here is that a trust wants to meet a particular need or solve a particular problem. Funding your organisation or your work may be a way of meeting this need. Giving you a grant is a means to an end, not an end in itself. The trust is interested in what will change, and for whom, as a result of the funding it gives your group for your project.

Type of activities the trust is willing to support

Some trusts are willing to support a wide range of activities. Others make it clear that there are some activities they will not fund. Some provide a list of the types of activities they will consider. Such activities might include events, pilot projects, research or training, for example.

Usually trusts will be clear about whether or not they will fund building work (capital projects).

A community project, working with young people, applied successfully to a trust for funding for a dance project to encourage self-expression and raise self-esteem. These outcomes could have been achieved by a different process – such as group discussions, training, or outward bound activities. However, these other activities would not have been funded by the trust that focused on the use of arts in personal development.

Approaches

A trust might be interested in the method of approach to your work. In other words, they are looking at the way something is done, rather than the activity or outcomes.

This can include things like partnership working, user involvement and being able to demonstrate that you are practising equal opportunities.

Types of funding

A trust might give one or more types of funding.

- **Short term 'firestarting' funding** – to get a project off the ground ('pump priming').
- **Revenue** – to cover the running costs of a project, including salaries.
- **Capital funding** – for building, refurbishment and items of equipment.
- **Project funding** – for a mix of elements, sometimes including a contribution to the organisation's overheads in respect of resources provided to the project. The funding could be for a fixed period of three to five years.
- **Core/long-term funding** – a few trusts provide some charities with core-funding for their work, or funding for specific projects or centres of excellence, over a number of years. A close partnership can develop, and the trust can build up joint expertise with the charity working on the ground.
- **Small grants** – some trusts only provide small grants; others offer this option as part of their grant making. Usually the procedures involved in applying for small sums of money are simpler than those for larger grants. Your application will still be carefully vetted. But the paperwork and length of time involved will usually be less. Trusts recognise the need for small grants to developing grassroots organisations – so some of the largest grant makers operate small grants programmes.

Eligible organisations

Trusts do not accept applications from all types of organisation.

They usually consider requests from:

- registered charities;
- community/voluntary organisations carrying out 'charitable work'. In some cases any funding received may need to go through a third party (registered charity) or other recognised body (such as a university).

Area of geographical benefit

Many trusts are set up to support groups working within a particular geographical area of benefit. They might focus on one or more towns or counties. The area of benefit and the location of your organisation need not necessarily be the same.

In fact, some of the large trusts have preferred geographical areas of benefit. All trusts will have policies on whether or not they support international, or overseas, work.

Size of grant

Trusts have different amounts of money to give away in any one year. But the size of individual grants won't always directly reflect the size of the trust itself.

Some smaller trusts might give just one or two relatively large grants each year.

Large trusts do not always give out large amounts of money per grant. Often they have a mixed programme of grant making, combining large grants and smaller sums.

A small community food project run by people with mental health problems managed to get off the ground, thanks to a development grant from a national trust. The group had been running informally up until this point and did not have a bank account or written constitution. The trust made its grant through the local council of voluntary service. With the trust funding, the group came together formally as a charity, and put together a plan for the next three years. The trust made a further grant – directly to the charity – a year later. And this helped the group to buy and equip its premises.

Funding period

A trust might be willing to fund a project over a year. Some will give grants for up to a maximum of three years. Some may be willing to renew their funding after this period, but only if the demand to continue can be clearly demonstrated. They may provide funds for the project to move on to a new phase of development, or activity. A handful of trusts will look at funding over five years, or for longer periods.

Funding a building, of course, has a more long-term impact on a charity. Owning premises, rather than paying rent, can save an organisation a substantial sum over the years. Some of the larger trusts are prepared to fund buildings as part of an overall long-term development plan.

Financial and management capability

Trusts always consider the financial soundness of any organisation seeking funds. Often they ask to see your most recent signed and approved annual accounts, as appropriate to your legal status.

Financial position

From this they can see whether what you spent last year was less or equal to the funds you received. If the accounts show a deficit, they will want to be reassured that this is being taken seriously, and to understand how this is being addressed. They will not give you money simply to fund a deficit which, after all, is for work that has already happened.

If there is a surplus then they will check to see the level of reserves you have – if you're lucky enough to have any! They will want to know what the money is in reserve for. You may be committing some of this to the project in hand, but you will need to explain this. You will probably have money in reserve for sound management reasons, and the Charity Commission has said that it is reasonable to have up to 12 months running costs in reserve. The important thing is to explain clearly what this money is for, rather than leaving it as an unexplained item.

A surplus or a deficit both say something about your ability to manage money.

Management capacity

Accounts will prompt a trust to review your management capacity.

For instance, a small organisation with an income of £10,000 per year might make an application for £100,000 to employ three staff running training workshops across the county. A trust would ask: 'Can this organisation go from no staff to three staff overnight? Who will manage them, and how? Is this realistic? What happens at the end of the project?'

You need to be able to show that you have thought through the implications of your project, can properly resource it, and put any necessary management structures in place.

Sensible budgeting

A trust will look to see whether or not your budget is based on reasonable costs – and is not over-inflated or impossibly small.

What won't trusts fund?

Some trusts see themselves as filling a gap – between what the state will fund and what the community needs. Others see themselves as funders of the unpopular, the risky, or the innovative. There are trusts that give grants to independent schools and hospitals, but generally trusts are not keen to provide money to work which they think should be state-funded.

If a local authority has funded a project or organisation over a number of years and then cuts its budget, few trusts will step in. Some are prepared to help if the organisation or project can survive for a year or more after the local authority funding has stopped. Such provision is sometimes described as 'additionality'.

They will need to be convinced that their money isn't a straight substitute for local authority funding.

> A welfare advice organisation had been running a rural outreach service for the past five years. This had been funded by grants from the local county council. However, the county went through a round of budget cutbacks and ended its support for the project. The group approached a dozen different trusts and got turned down by them all. It received feedback from three of the trusts who all said that they were unwilling to fill the gap left by the local authority – they felt that it sent a signal that councils could simply cut their budgets and expect trusts to meet the difference. Sadly the group didn't find another funder for the service and had to stop this part of its work.

Trusts won't generally fund a commercial organisation or project. The funding should be for a charitable purpose.

Most important of all, trusts won't fund anything which is outside their trust deed or funding policy. Trusts won't usually fund work retrospectively – that is they won't pay for work that has already been completed. The majority of trusts will not repay a loan that was taken out to run a project – by implication, the organisation believes it can repay the loan, as does the lender. One or two trusts may consider being the lender.

Why would a trust fund your work?

Try to think about your organisation and your work from the trust's perspective. This will help you to assess whether or not you have any chance of securing their support.

It's all too easy to be full of enthusiasm for your organisation or project and to think that you deserve a grant. Instead, it is more appropriate to think in the following terms.

- **Achieving the trust's purpose** – can you explain how your work will help the trust to achieve its purpose?
- **Meeting funding policies, priorities and criteria** – are you able to meet all of the trust's stated policies, priorities and criteria? Have you read any published guidelines?

A charity applied to a trust for a grant to develop a housing project for people with mental health problems. The charity was able to demonstrate a clear need for the project, with evidence of the difference the work could make. However, the fundraiser requested £50,000 from a trust that clearly stated that its grants were up to a maximum of £5,000. The application was turned down.

The fundraiser also approached a trust that funded projects in one particular county – the project was based in another. The application was turned down.

The fundraiser sent an application to a trust that said it did not want to receive unsolicited applications. He never had a response.

First things first

Before you can approach any trusts, you need to prepare your case for funding – being clear about what it is you want money for and why. We are going to look at making the case for funding in the next chapter.

Making the case for funding

In this chapter you will find out about the importance of:

▶ Defining the work you want a trust to support

▶ Developing a 'project' structure – and how to do so

▶ Making the case for your project – and how to justify the need for the work you are proposing

Defining your work as a 'project'

Research into the patterns of grant making (*Dimensions 2000*) found that donations for social care, education, arts and the environment are dominated by grants for projects. Funding for capital work dominated grants under the heading 'religion'. And the sciences received grants largely for research. Even capital or building work and research could be presented as a 'project', as we will see below.

It is important to pull your plans together as a 'project', rather than a wish list of things you need, because:

- funding is often time-limited and you need to show what will be achieved during the lifetime of the grant;
- many trusts won't consider core-funding an organisation. A discrete project can be supported with less risk that at the end of the grant the organisation will be dependent on its funder;
- a project structure provides evidence of planning – and that means you are more likely to turn your ideas and proposals into real achievements.

Some people find it difficult to translate their ideas into a project structure. It might be helpful to consider a project as a piece of work that takes place over a limited time period. There should be a clear beginning and end to the work. You will be able to say at the outset what you hope to achieve over the coming months or years. At the end of the work, you will be able to review what has actually been done.

Why you need to make your case

Only by making the case for your project will you be clear about things such as:

- the levels of need or demand for your work, with evidence to support any claims;
- the different goals you have for your project, which can be measured throughout the life of the project;
- the people you are trying to reach, and how you will extend opportunities to those who are under-represented or disadvantaged;
- detailed costs and timings;
- the sustainability or future development of the project.

Not only will *you* be clear about the above, but you will be able to demonstrate certain facts or evidence to colleagues and potential funders.

Once you have this sort of information you will be able to look at who might consider funding such work. You will be able to plan to approach specific funders.

And this document will also be your starting point for a fundraising application. You will be able to draw on the information to write applications, drawing out appropriate elements for different funders. It will be a handy reference point if you are interviewed or visited by a trust as part of the assessment process.

What to include when you make your case

There are a number of elements that you should include when you are outlining the case for your project.

- **Introduction** – to give context and an overview (just because you are extremely familiar with your work and its value, don't assume that other people, even within your own organisation, will be).
- **About your organisation** – this information will outline your experience and expertise, in effect saying why you, rather than someone else, should be doing the work.
- **The project** – this section gets to the heart of what it is you intend to do.
- **Justification** – in this section you explain why your project is a good solution to a particular problem, or how it meets a need.
- **The process** – here you explain how users will be involved, the role of partners, how you will react and how you will reach the people in need. You will also describe the resources you require (people and materials), when and where you will make the project happen, and why.

- **Costs and funding** – you will work through the project budget and opportunities for funding (from different sources).
- **The end of the project** – this also needs to be considered. What you are planning to do when the initial funding ceases? Will the project end on a set date, or be self-sustaining?

The above elements should be set out in this order in your proposal, even though you might gather information and evidence in a different sequence. For instance, the justification for your project is the reason why you want to do the work. However, in making your case, you outline the project first and then provide the evidence behind the need.

Let's look at each of these headings in a bit more detail below.

Project proposal: introduction

In your introduction you should explain how the project came about. Has it evolved over time or has it been suggested by users of your service? Perhaps it's the result of a collaboration with other organisations, or it might have come to you in a flash of inspiration.

If the project has come from out of the blue it doesn't mean it isn't needed, but you are going to have to do some work to show that there is a demand, or why it's needed. And we'll return to this issue when we look at 'justification'.

You can also explain, in your introduction, who is involved in the work. Is it your group working alone, or are you working in partnership with some other organisations?

The introduction is a good place to give an idea of the timescales involved. And it's an opportunity to say how this particular project fits in with the rest of your work, and your organisation's objectives.

Project proposal: about your organisation

The next area to cover is your own organisation. This may feel like going over old ground – explaining things you already know. However, when you come to approach potential funders you will need this information – presented clearly and positively.

Setting out this information now will enable you to reproduce this section in full or in part when you make your trust applications.

Your roots

You should provide a very brief (three or four line) overview of your organisation's development – if you have been going for some years this could show that you are an established and experienced group. If you are relatively new then you obviously represent a grassroots response to an emerging need!

Outline the reason for your organisation's existence – this should reflect why you are proposing the particular piece of work. You might want to refer to the purpose of your group as outlined in your original constitution. If your current work has changed substantially from your constitution you might need to think about updating it. Your local council of voluntary service and the Charity Commission can both provide guidance on how to do this. Funders are naturally nervous of any proposals that do not fit the words and spirit of an organisation's constitution. This in itself might lead to your application being turned down.

What you are doing now

It's worth including a brief overview of what you are involved with at the moment. And you should also list up to three things that you've recently achieved – things that demonstrate your expertise and approach. You need to be clear about what kind of organisation you are – all trusts will want to know this and some limit the kinds of organisations they are willing to support.

Your status

You might be a charitable organisation; a company limited by guarantee; or a registered charity, for instance. Some trusts will be willing to fund more informal emergent groups by giving their funds to an umbrella organisation, such as a council of voluntary service, to hold on the new group's behalf.

Your financial status

You will need to show most potential funders copies of your annual report and accounts – from at least the previous year.

Make a note of your annual income and expenditure over the past three years, commenting on any surplus or deficit.

As we said in the previous chapter, trusts will want to know why you are holding reserves. If this applies to you, you will need to say why the reserves aren't all being used to support the project you are asking others to fund. Also be ready to explain anything unusual in your accounts.

You may want to include details of the current financial state of your organisation, taken from your management accounts or current statement of income and expenditure. And accompany these with the projected figures to the end of the year, if you have them. Make a note for yourself of any financial issues that might arise before the year-end – for example how you plan to deal with a delay in receiving funds, or a decision on a grant.

Project proposal: the project itself

We have talked in terms of a project because this is what most funders are looking for. Replacing a building, a special trip, or buying a new item of equipment can all be described as a project. A project is a plan of work or action, with aims and objectives, a clear timetable of action, and a beginning, middle and end (see below).

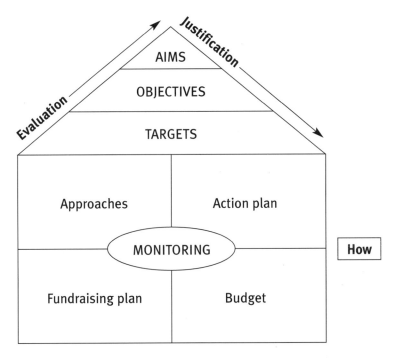

A project has aims and objectives, outlining how you will make a difference to the lives of people who will benefit.

You need to be thinking in this frame of mind when applying to a grant-making trust. They will be looking at the impact of their grants on individuals and local communities. You will probably address this issue through your project aims and objectives.

For example, a trust might be asked to fund a boathouse – but why would they? They might consider supporting the work if there are clear aims and objectives that match their own funding priorities. One trust might fund a boathouse that provides disadvantaged young people with a chance to learn valuable social and practical skills. Another trust might fund a boathouse if it provides leisure activities for older disabled people as a means of reducing their isolation. It's about making a difference to people's lives, not the building itself.

Whether you are putting together a proposal for a three-year project involving hundreds of people or for the purchase of a piece of equipment, you should be able to say a few words under each of the following headings.

Aims and objectives

You will probably want to begin with a simple statement of why you are doing the work – what is it you are hoping to achieve or change?

Your aim for the project should outline what changes you want to bring about, and for whom, as a result of the project. The aim may also try to define just how much change you hope to make.

Your objectives for the project should explain what the beneficiaries will be able to do that they could not before. To describe how this will happen, you need to define some targets – things that you are able to measure to confirm that the beneficiaries can do what you expected at the end of the project, that is you have achieved the results you wanted.

An organisation for Deaf people was concerned about barriers preventing proper access to health and welfare services. They put together a project with the following aim, objectives and targets.

Aim: we want to improve the access of Deaf people in our county to health and welfare advice and services.

Objectives: we want to:

- raise the awareness of doctors, social workers and other professionals of the access needs of Deaf people, along with the implications of the Disability Discrimination Act;
- bring Deaf people together with health and welfare professionals to improve communications and establish regular consultation;
- develop a range of appropriate support services for local Deaf people.

Targets: we intend to:

- hold a county-wide conference for 100 people, and a series of five local seminars for up to 25 people at each (September–March);
- create a consultative forum which continues the dialogue between local Deaf people and health and welfare professionals. The first forum will take place within two months of the final seminar, and will then meet quarterly;
- set up a user support network, providing advice and information to local Deaf people. The network would offer a part-time helpline (weekday mornings) and advice desk at the monthly Deaf Club;
- develop a communications resource, providing details of interpreters, lip-speakers and other communications aids for health and welfare professionals.

Target audience: Deaf people, health and welfare professionals.

Project proposal: justification

The justification part of your planning is essential if you are going to convince any trusts to fund your work. It's easy to be so close to a project that you take it for granted that the work should happen.

You should take a step back and explain why the project is needed. You might want to do something, but you must be able to demonstrate that you need to do it or that there is a problem to solve.

You may already have all the information at your fingertips to put together a convincing argument. You might have to conduct some research to gather the evidence.

Strategic needs

You could refer to evidence produced at a strategic level. This is information gathered for a wider area than that covered by your project. It will support your arguments about the need for your project. And it helps to show that what you are planning complements the work of local government and other agencies. Similarly, these organisations might have produced strategic plans outlining how they propose to meet community-wide needs. You can again strengthen your case by showing how your project helps to deliver the outcomes outlined in these plans.

Evidence might be produced at strategic level by your local authority, an umbrella voluntary organisation, or a network of community groups. There might be one or more strategic plans that you can refer to – showing how your project could help to meet these community-wide priorities. You can find out this sort of information by getting in touch with your local council, or by visiting your local library.

> The local Deaf organisation described above had some national research to show the need for action.
>
> Almost a quarter of Deaf and hard of hearing people leave a doctor's surgery without knowing what is wrong with them. Almost a third depend on family or friends to interpret when finding out about health and welfare. One in six avoid going to their GP because of the barriers to effective communication.

Direct need

Next, you should show the direct need for your service. This might be at a local level, and it will certainly reflect the impact you hope to make on your clients or beneficiaries. You need to be able to back up any claims you make such as '100 of our clients have said that they would use a service of this kind'. Do you have the results of a survey to prove the point? Have you carried out any pilot projects to test reaction?

> The local Deaf organisation which wanted to set up a health and welfare project had conducted its own client/user survey. This showed that the situation in their county was worse than the national survey suggested. Half of the Deaf people who visited a doctor's surgery left without knowing what was wrong with them. Two thirds had no idea of their welfare entitlements, and when they tried to find out about their rights a quarter used a friend or family member to interpret for them.

Some of the ways you might demonstrate direct client need include:

- a feasibility study;
- a client/user survey;
- a pilot project.

Feasibility study

A feasibility study can help to:

- establish what your current clients or service users want;
- show how your project fits with the work of other organisations, and any strategic or development plans;

- explore wider community needs;
- firm up the scope and scale of the project;
- set some broad goals;
- establish new networks and contacts;
- discover ways of reaching different harder-to-reach or under-represented groups.

Client/user survey

A survey can provide evidence directly from your clients or service users. And it might be extended to potential users. Questionnaires need to be put together carefully and tested out for any ambiguity or confusing questions. One way of ensuring you have a clear questionnaire, written in an appropriate way, is to involve users in its creation.

If you are using postal surveys, don't forget to say whether or not the questionnaire is anonymous. And include a return address and phone number. You will get a higher response rate (and it might be more appropriate for your users) if you include a pre-paid envelope for their reply.

You might carry out a survey through postal questionnaires, by running through questions with people face-to-face or over the phone, or by working with small focus groups. In focus groups, you can ask a representative group of people about their particular needs and suggested solutions. You can test out ideas and receive some practical feedback from the people who would use your services.

Before working with a focus group you need to be clear about how you will ensure that participants are truly representative of your client or user group. And you will need to explain this along with the results of the focus group.

You should always publish the findings of such a survey with details of how you intend to build on the results, so that people can see that their responses have been put to good use.

Pilot project

A pilot project can demonstrate how people are likely to respond to a project in action. They allow you to test out different approaches, and see what people think in practice.

Working together

You have so far worked from your project outwards – looking for evidence that your project is needed. You should also take a community-wide perspective. Are there other local agencies working in the local community who have identified gaps that your project may help to fill? Could they work with you to help you (and them) achieve more than either of you could alone?

You might, for instance, find that your local council has a community development plan that highlights some particular gaps or priorities. These could be partially met by your project. Perhaps your local council of voluntary service has identified a particular need that you can address through your work. By asking the question you might identify some other sources of funding.

It is also worth considering whether there are any other organisations addressing similar or complementary issues. Could you work together on this project to avoid duplication and increase your effectiveness?

Project proposal: the process

The 'process' is a plan of action for the delivery of your project. You might want to start by giving an idea of your general approach before focusing on the step-by-step work that is needed to carry out the project.

Approaches

If you are working in partnership with other organisations, then you should explain how this will work. What particular roles and responsibilities will be undertaken by each partner?

You will need to explain how you intend to reach your client group. How, for example, will you reach under-represented groups? How will you show that your project will be open to all? You might, for instance, produce posters in large print, or in different languages. You might employ a female outreach worker to work with women from a particular culture.

You should also say how you plan to involve and represent your client group in the project. You might involve clients in management, monitoring and research.

And you should outline how you will ensure equality of opportunity in the way you recruit and employ staff and volunteers to work on the project.

Your action plan

You've already said why you are doing the project in your aims, objectives and targets. Now you need to explain:

- who will do it? (people)
- what will they do? (actions)
- when will they do it? (times)

- where will they do it? (places)
- how will they do it? (process)
- how will you tell how well they did it? (monitoring and evaluation)

This is your action plan. It describes what resources you will need, and how you will use them in a practical way. This will be the starting point for working out your budget.

The people

You need to be clear about who is coordinating the project. This might mean that the first step in the process is to appoint a project organiser.

You may need to recruit and train volunteers to work on the project.

Actions

You could describe the different actions as they will happen – starting with initial research, moving on to preparation, then promotion and so on. You might want to put this information together as a timetable or Gantt chart.

Times

A timetable of action will run through the different actions under monthly or weekly headings.

A Gantt chart allows you to show at a glance how long each element takes, specific dates to note and important milestones as well as when things will happen. You can see how delays to one element affect the whole.

In a Gantt chart you list the different elements down the left hand side of the table and the months or weeks across the top (see below).

	January	February	March	April
Agree programme	12th			
Produce publicity materials				
Recruit volunteers				
Training events			1st 8th	3rd 15th

You can also be more general and talk about months or weeks one, two, three and so on, instead of giving actual months. This might be appropriate if you are approaching some of the trusts that make decisions more infrequently. They might be put off if they see a looming deadline, or one that looks as though it has passed. Instead, you might want to show that the project can start as soon as all funds are in place.

Places

You should explain where the work will take place, indicating the boundaries within which you are working. You should say whether or not you need a venue or meeting place for the project.

Monitoring and evaluation

You should explain how you plan to track your progress, and evaluate your achievements.

Monitoring

Monitoring is about asking:

- how does what we said we'd do compare with what we've done? why?
- what else do we need to do to meet our targets?
- do we need to do some things differently to meet our targets?

It helps you to see how you are progressing, and to change course, if necessary, to ensure the project succeeds.

You might gather figures or 'quantitative information' – about numbers of people involved, and their achievements. These are statistics that can demonstrate how many people you have supported.

Numbers alone are not enough, however. You will also want to find out how people feel about your work – this is 'qualitative information'. It can tell you about how well your approach is working, and how the users/clients perceive the benefits of your project.

Monitoring provides evidence of the process and results – it's like building up a photo album, or record of events.

Monitoring is about comparing what you set out to do with what you have in fact achieved. You can also easily confirm which things in your action plan have been completed, and when. Gathering this information will enable you to start thinking about how well the project is succeeding. You may need to change your plan to make sure that targets are met.

Evaluation

Evaluation is about judging how well the project has achieved its purpose by asking:

- how well did we meet our objectives? why?
- to what extent have we met our aims? why?

It means you need to work with users after the work has ended to determine how their lives have changed because of the project. Commissioning an independent evaluation may be worth considering, and this will need to be provided for in your budget. The evaluation can become a starting point to develop your future plans for the project.

Project proposal: costs and funding

The next part of your case is the budget.

When you approach a trust you are asking for a contribution towards actual costs. This is very different from asking a company for sponsorship. Sponsorship involves asking the company to pay for the value of your project to them – this could be two or three times the actual direct costs.

A trust will want to see a detailed budget, along with your accounts throughout the life of the project to prove you have spent the money as promised.

Your budget should be based on your action plan. It needs to be well thought through, and not inflated. The figures should look sensible, and should cover all the costs. If you put in a sum as a contingency you should say what sort of eventualities it might be needed for. Trusts are unlikely to give money away to cover 'the unknown'.

Your budget for year one of the project should be as detailed as possible. You should also include projections for years two and three, if your project continues into the future.

State clearly any assumptions you are making – such as any income you anticipate from other sources.

Your budget will need to relate to the process you have already described. It can be laid out in many ways, for example using the following headings.

People

When you are outlining the cost of people working on the project you might give details of salaries, with National Insurance contributions included. Or you may have volunteer expenses.

Overheads

Workers on the project may be based within the office of your organisation. So, they may benefit from the core team who do the accounts, pay the wages, carry out secretarial work and so on, as well as from the organisation's insurance policies, and other central services. You will therefore need to calculate the proportion of your organisation's general overheads to put against a particular project.

> A multi-cultural organisation wanted to set up a lunch club for older members of minority ethnic communities. The work involved a new part-time post, supported by the rest of the five-person team. The charity calculated that the part-time worker accounted for about one tenth of their office space (rent and rates); and five per cent of central services (insurance, accounting and administrative support). They added this to the cost of the direct project budget (which included room hire, refreshments and transport). The charity showed this item as a heading in their budget so that it was clear to any potential funders.

There are a number of trusts who won't pay towards this element. However, it is a real cost and will need to be covered – even if this is a contribution your organisation makes towards the project out of general funds. If the project represents the total work of your organisation, you will need the same figures.

Running costs

The running costs of your project might be little more than the salaries of the workers and the overheads involved. But they could be much bigger – involving the hire of other premises, production of print and other materials, vehicle running costs and so on. You may need to buy services from, for instance, an accountant (professional fees) or buy in the services of contract or feelance staff for short periods. Many trusts will consider funding project running costs as well as capital items.

Capital costs

If the project involves the purchase of equipment, buildings or land, then they come under the broad heading of 'capital'. Some trusts fund only the capital elements of a project. This will probably include the building or equipment itself, along with the planning and development work involved. Other trusts never fund capital elements of a project.

Capital projects can be complex. If there is a building or refurbishment involved, make sure you take appropriate advice before making a commitment. Costs can increase significantly later on if you fail to plan ahead and get professional help at the right time.

Trusts which fund capital projects do so because of what will be achieved by having the building – a means to an end. You will need to work up income and expenditure projections for at least three years from when the building is ready for use – showing that it can be self-sufficient and will not constantly rely on grants to stay open.

In this way you demonstrate that the building will not turn out to be a white elephant. You will also need to indicate the long-term future for work within the building.

Anticipated income

You might have some more or less guaranteed sources of income – including a contribution from your own reserves. These should be outlined within your budget. You will be fundraising for the difference between expenditure and income.

In the past some charities have made the mistake of either:

- inflating their budgets – thinking that a trust would 'top slice' them and only offer up to 90 per cent; or
- under-costing – thinking that they should make their costs look as low as possible, to increase their chances of funding.

Both approaches are mistaken, because most trusts appreciate how much a project should cost. They receive hundreds of applications so they are in a good position to take such a view. Your application might well be turned down if you are significantly over or under budget, since:

- if you over-budget then the value for money (cost per person who benefits) will be higher than other similar applications – you might therefore be turned down;
- if you under-budget then the trust might think that you can't cost things accurately and the project is likely to fail – you might therefore be turned down.

A trust may offer you less than you asked for because you have over-budgeted. Or it may simply wish to participate at a different level.

The key point is that if a project is worth doing and you are the right people to do it, then you should be able to find someone to support it at this level. Don't be ashamed or embarrassed by the costs.

Fundraising

Once you have outlined your anticipated expenditure you need to work out how to raise the necessary income.

You need to describe:

- who is responsible for raising the money;
- income targets;
- a fundraising timetable;
- the mix of funders for this particular project.

Who is responsible for raising the money?

One person within your organisation needs to take overall responsibility for the fundraising. However, just because it falls to an individual (probably to you) there's no need for fundraising to be a lonely business. You can benefit greatly from a quick brainstorm with friends, colleagues, or fundraisers from other groups.

Income targets

Your budget will give you an idea of the overall income target. However, you might want to stage this over time – for years one, two and three, for instance. Or you might want to break the total figure into smaller sums per funder. For example, your budget might be £4,000. But you might want to try to raise five grants each worth around £800.

Your fundraising timetable

You need to set a fundraising timetable so that you have a clear sense of direction, and so that you can measure progress – see below. There may come a point when you have to say: 'Right, that's it, I've spent too much time on this, we aren't going to raise the necessary money, so let's think again.'

Source £	Amount requested (£)	Submitted by (date)	Response by (date)	Outcome (£)
Our reserves	2,000	N/A	N/A	2,000
Widgets Ltd	3,000	March 00	June 00	
Maple Charitable Trust	500	April 00	Aug 00	
Cherry Foundation	10,000	April 00	Sept 00	

The mix of funders for this particular project

You need to describe the funding mix for the project. Each project is different. Some are more appropriate for company sponsorship. Some are right for local government support, or a grant from a quango. You need to think about whether you are going to focus on one or more different types of funder.

More often than not, a potential funder will want to know what sort of funding mix you hope to achieve for a project. They might ask whether or not they will be the only funder. They might consider whether you have contributed some money to the project from your reserves. They might look to see if your local council is willing to provide some financial backing.

Project proposal: the end of the project

The end of your project may seem quite a way off, but many funders want to know that you are thinking about what might happen once their grant has finished – they won't be able to fund you forever. They don't want to raise expectations that cannot be met.

'Exit strategies' (see page 59) describe how you plan to ensure you don't leave a gap – people without services or facilities that they have come to expect as a result of your project. This is what some funders call 'sustainability'.

Some trusts provide grants which 'taper' over time to help organisations gradually find funding from other sources.

It is very important for you to explain clearly how your project is likely to continue into the future, or how it will achieve its goals within a limited time. If a trust thinks you will be dependent on it for funding and a project might collapse at the end of the grant, then it probably won't support your project. Here are some examples of how a project might continue in the future.

- **The project might finish on a set date** – it could be that the project has a natural lifespan of one or more years, particularly if it is a building project, an event, or a pilot piece of work. The learning might then be disseminated to others at the end of the work.
- **The project might become self-funding** – after the initial phase your project might generate its own income in the future, becoming self-financing.
- **You might find new funding partners** – as a project develops, new partners might be sought to continue or develop the work. Your funding plan might have identified where these partners will come from.
- **New projects or activities evolve** – new initiatives might grow out of the existing project to meet new and changing needs. Funding could come from established and new sources.

What are trusts looking for?

Grant-making trusts will usually be looking for some sort of exit strategy when they assess your application. This means that they want to know what you plan to do when their financial support runs out (an indication of what might happen at the end of the project). Clearly it can only be an intention at this stage, but it will affect how you manage your project and, therefore, its success or failure. Most only give grants for limited periods of time, although some provide longer-term support. Trusts want to make an impact with their funding. And sometimes this can be achieved within a set time frame.

Trusts do not want to appear to put some money into a project which is initially a fantastic success but then suddenly ceases. To the outside world it will appear that they have withdrawn money, causing a project to collapse, even if in fact they only ever had a limited commitment to it. They are very concerned about how such an eventuality could affect staff at the project and the communities that benefit from it.

Room for change

Despite all this careful planning, there should always be room for creative experimentation and unexpected outcomes. It's what makes the voluntary sector exciting, and more responsive to people's needs.

Where to get advice and help

The kind of planning described in this chapter becomes easier with practical experience. Once you have worked on several projects you get a feel for realistic timetabling, things to watch out for in the budget and so on. If this is one of your first projects, you might want to find further advice and help.

Experienced colleagues

Some of your colleagues or committee members might have previous experience of project proposals. This might have been within the voluntary sector, or in another environment – for a company or local authority. It's always worth asking around within your own organisation before looking for outside help.

Expert volunteers or secondees

You might want to recruit a volunteer to help with your project proposals. Your local volunteer bureau (listed in the phone book or in the directory produced by the National Association of Volunteer Bureaux) might be able to help. There are also volunteer organisations for retired people (more likely to have such experience) – these include RSVP (Retired Senior Volunteer Programme) and REACH (Retired Excecutives Action Clearing House). Contact details for NAVB, RSVP and REACH are listed in *Further information*.

You might also benefit from the assistance of a secondee. Some companies support charities and community groups by providing members of staff on a short- or medium-term basis (whilst still paying their salaries). From the company's point of view it is a way of developing their employees' skills, involving them in new and challenging environments. The secondee can gain new skills. And the community group can gain a valuable business perspective. This all depends on the right people being placed with the right community groups. As with any volunteer, you will need a job description and an interview process to ensure things work well.

An extra and experienced person can save you time. However, they might not know your organisation's work and approach as well as your existing staff and volunteers. Some people might feel that recruiting someone to help with project planning and fundraising is not the most effective use of volunteers.

> A small group set up by the families of children with drug and alcohol problems wanted to provide more support services. For years it had been run from people's homes, and with very little income. A local business offered the charity an office within its building, and one of its managers to provide part-time marketing and development support. The seconded manager worked with the group's director to make the case for an expansion of its work, including the appointment of a full-time administrator. She also helped the charity's director to write a funding plan for this development. The director then went on to make several successful applications to trusts and businesses for support.

Other charities

Workers from other charities can be very helpful, with down-to-earth advice. They might have some examples of project proposals for you to look at. But they are pressed for time, just like you.

Training

There are training courses on project management. These are available from commercial, as well as not-for-profit, organisations. The Directory of Social Change also runs some workshops on this theme (see *Further information* for contact details).

Some companies might be prepared for you to attend staff training, as a way of making a contribution. However, don't expect them to do the fundraising for you.

Professional fundraisers

You might want to consult a professional fundraiser or project management expert. They can help you to translate your ideas into practical steps. The Institute of Charity Fundraising Managers and National Council for Voluntary Organisations can tell you more about professional fundraisers.

Consultants can help you sort out ideas and structure your project. But funders prefer to hear about it in your own words.

If they want to know more, you will be best-placed to tell them about the project, and if funded it is you who's going to build the relationship with a trust. Trusts are interested in good projects, not just well-presented ones!

Charity information bureaux and advice services

There are a number of organisations set up to give fundraising advice and support to voluntary groups. Some describe themselves as a charity information bureau or a charity advice service. You can find out if there is one in your area by contacting the Federation of Charity Advice Services (FCAS); details are in *Further information*.

Voluntary sector development agencies

Finally, you may be able to get practical advice and help from your local council of voluntary service or similar development agency. If you don't have details of your local CVS you can contact the National Association of Councils of Voluntary Service (NACVS) (details in *Further information*) or look in your local phone book. And at a national level organisations such as the National Council for Voluntary Organisations and Charities Aid Foundation can also provide useful help and advice.

Ready to go

Once you have made the case for your project, you are ready to research the relevant grant-making trusts. Only when you are clear on the detail of what you are trying to raise money for can you move forward with your research.

Researching appropriate trusts

In this chapter we look at:

▶ The importance of matching what you plan to do with a trust's objectives
▶ Where to find out information about particular trusts
▶ What to look for when you are researching trusts
▶ How to create a hit-list of trusts to approach

Finding the fit

Fundraising from grant-making trusts is about showing the match between what a trust wants to achieve (through its funding) and what you can deliver (through your work). It therefore follows that the closer the fit between the trust's stated policies, priorities or criteria and your project the more likely you are to succeed in securing funds. Given the vast differences between trusts you are only going to achieve this fit with a well-researched, targeted approach.

Over the past few months, or years, you might have compiled a database of information on trusts as, and when, you found out about them – if they could be relevant to your work. Or you could be starting from scratch.

In either case, you will probably want to do some more intensive research into relevant trusts when you have made the case for your project.

At this stage you will be clear about what you want to raise money for. And you will know the key facts such as: who will benefit from the project; where they will be based; what needs are being addressed; and how much money you are looking for. All of these issues, and more, will determine who you should approach for support.

Using available information

You may be able to draw on the information you currently have in your fundraising database, and in your files. But you will need to look elsewhere for further information – and it exists in various places.

Trusts themselves

Trusts publish different degrees of information about what they are trying to achieve through their grants. The information might be produced as a set of guidelines or brief summary, or be included in the trust's annual report and accounts, lodged with the Charity Commission. Trusts such as the City Parochial Foundation, Paul Hamlyn Foundation and Gulbenkian Foundation produce clear guidelines for potential applicants.

Trusts themselves provide the information that is included in *The Directory of Grant Making Trusts* (see page 48).

What others publish

There are a variety of databases and directories published by third party organisations. These list trusts in a variety of ways – according to the level of funds they distribute; their geographical coverage; and the areas of work in which they are interested, for instance. Your local reference library and CVS are both good places to start if you don't want to buy books initially. We describe published resources in more detail below.

Other sources of information

You can find out information from a variety of other sources – your colleagues, advice agencies, firms of solicitors and so on. Word of mouth information can be incredibly valuable. You can find out useful contact details, information about previously funded projects, and anecdotal details of the kind of work the trustees prefer.

What do you want to achieve?

By the end of your research you should have the following.

- **A list of trusts worth approaching** – we've called this a 'hit-list'. Your hit-list should pick out those trusts whose aims can be achieved through your project. The aim is to write to a few relevant trusts.
- **A heightened chance of success** – if you identify a dozen or so trusts that look fairly promising, and perhaps a couple with more of an outside chance, then you are likely to have a higher success rate. And you are less likely to need to do some more frantic fundraising to fill the gap.
- **Cost-effective results** – your research should save you time, effort and postage in the long-run. It might seem easier to send off a mail-merged letter

to the first 50 trusts on your database. You may feel better now because you are carrying out a sizeable task, but think about how you will feel when you hear nothing or get lots of rejection letters. It's quality, not quantity, that counts.

How are you going to do it?

First you should be clear about what you need to find out about different trusts. It's relatively easy to find out their address and a contact person, but what else do you need to know before you can prepare an approach?

What you need to know

You need to know what is guiding a trust when it makes decisions on grant applications – their decision-making framework, as we described it in Chapter 3. In other words, you need to find out as much as you can about:

- the problems or needs in which the trust is interested;
- the type of activities the trust is willing to support;
- any particular ways of working (or methodologies) the trust has prioritised;
- types of funding the trust is willing to consider;
- restrictions on the type of organisation the trust will fund;
- the geographical area that the trust focuses on;
- the size of grant the trust is able to give;
- the length of time the trust will support a project;
- policies relating to financial matters, e.g. reserves or income levels of applicant organisation.

This information will enable you to see if there is a 'fit' between your project and the aims of the trust.

In addition, as part of your research, you should find out if any supporting paperwork is required; for example, an application form or proposal, annual report and accounts.

So, how can you find out this information? We have already said that the trusts themselves publish a certain amount of detail, but how do you know who they are in the first place? You need to use a range of resources.

Resources and sources of information

There are various resources that can help you in your search for information about different trusts. Always remember to read any written details in context – don't just lift out particular paragraphs or sentences that make a trust seem appropriate for your project. You need to consider all the available facts. And when you are using one of the directories read the instructions on how to use it – it will save you time and help you work more accurately. Further guidance on research is provided in *Find the Funds*, another 'How to' guide.

Paper-based directories

There are a number of useful directories published by the Directory of Social Change.

DSC has signed an agreement with the Charities Aid Foundation to research and publish future editions of *The Directory of Grant Making Trusts*. This directory is based on responses from trusts to draft entries produced by the researchers who compile the directory.

DSC also publishes *A Guide to the Major Trusts* in three volumes. Volume 1 covers the top 300 trusts, volume 2 outlines the next 700 major trusts, and volume 3 outlines a further 400 UK-wide trusts, plus grant makers in Scotland, Northern Ireland and Wales. There are also local guides for the South of England, the Midlands, the North of England and Greater London. These guides take a more in-depth and critical approach, and are not based solely on information provided by the trusts themselves.

Whatever the source of your information, always read the individual entry before making a final decision on whether or not to approach a particular trust.

And remember:

- you won't necessarily find the same information on the same trust in the different directories – additional information from other sources can help you refine your hit-list;
- information won't necessarily be up-to-date, so seek more if there's a contact number and if a trust publishes guidelines;
- be creative when you use the indices to directories. Trusts find it just as hard to categorise what they fund as you find it to categorise your project. No two charitable projects are exactly the same. The index categories only give you leads into trusts that may have an interest in your project. You are looking for what you have in common, so use the strongest defining factors to work through the index.

Paper-based directories can give you almost all the information you need to make an initial shortlist of relevant trusts. But you should always ring the trust for up-to-date information and guidelines (provided the trust has not stated that no phone contact should be made).

If the trust is happy to be contacted by phone, then you should ring them to check that you have the correct contact details (named person, and full address). You might also ask them for:

- the date of their next trustees' meeting, or specific deadlines for submissions;
- up-to-date details of their priorities, or a copy of any written guidance;
- a copy of any application form, or advice on the format of proposal they prefer to receive.

CD-ROMs and the Internet

You can also do some preliminary research by using CD-ROMs and the Internet. *The Directory of Grant Making Trusts* is available as the Grantseeker CD-ROM. You type in key words or information and the software sifts through its database to produce your shortlist of trusts. The Directory of Social Change publishes *The CD-ROM Trusts Guide* which includes all the data from the *Guide to the Major Trusts* volumes 1 and 2, and the four *Guides to the Local Trusts*. From 2001 both these CD-ROMs will be amalgamated into one useful database.

The popular CD FunderFinder complements the major paper-based directories, acting as a large database and referring to information published in the major guides. You can add relevant local information about your own area, and details of company giving and local authority funding. About half the 1,000 users of the FunderFinder software for 'Groups In Need' are development agencies, making the CD available to other groups. So it is worth asking your CVS if they have a copy for you to use.

FunderFinder also has a website at www.funderfinder.org.uk

The Internet itself is like a giant information database. And you can search for details of relevant trusts on-line.

Some trusts have their own websites, for instance:

- PPP Trust has a site at www.ppptrust.org
- the Baring Foundation can be found at www.baringfoundation.org.uk
- the Association of Charitable Foundations has a links page with direct pathways to trust sites. The ACF is at www.acf.org.uk

Other sites on the Internet provide helpful links and hints on fundraising from grant-making trusts. They include:

- www.vois.org.uk
- www.charitynet.org
- www.fundraising.co.uk
- www.dsc.org.uk

The Internet is a world-wide source of information. What can you do to help your search if you are looking much closer to home, for a very local trust?

Local development agencies

Your CVS or local authority might have produced a local directory of trusts. Even if they haven't developed a local listing, it's still worth talking to them. They might know of individual relevant trusts worth approaching.

Local research

Finally, you can carry out your own face-to-face research – asking for information from friends, colleagues and neighbours. It's also worth making contact with local firms of solicitors and accountants, who often administer small local trusts. You might contact your local authority, too, to see if they run any small hidden trusts.

Creating a hit-list

The resources and sources of information described above are just a starting point. Working from these you can reach a point where you have a hit-list of the best matches between your project and a particular trust. But there are different stages to go through on the way.

It's worth remembering that some trusts proactively approach the organisations they want to support. They state that they won't consider funding unsolicited applications. If this is the case then they should not appear on your hit-list of trusts to approach.

Create a long-list

To create your initial long-list, look first at the geographical area of benefit. If your project is in Cornwall, there's no point approaching a trust that focuses its funding on the Outer Hebrides. Of course, many trusts fund projects throughout the UK, or have a particular focus on England. Trusts with a wide geographical coverage are just as likely to appear on your long-list as those with a particular local focus. But you will rule some trusts out by looking at where they are willing to fund.

Next, look at the problems or needs in which the trust has an interest, and the target groups it wants to help. These may be defined in terms of 'fields of interest' and 'beneficiaries'. This information will start to give you an idea of those trusts working in similar areas to your organisation, and to this project.

At this stage you will have a long-list of trusts which might be interested in supporting your project. Some might be major trusts with a broad interest; others might be smaller, more focused trusts. You now need to narrow your list down and rule out some of these trusts.

Refine it into a short-list

Look at your long-list in as much detail as possible and check individual entries in the different directories or databases. Now remove any trusts that can't provide the sort of funding you are looking for – because your project does not match their priorities, or because of the size or length of grant you need, or the type of funding required. Check to see if your organisation is eligible to apply to each of the trusts on your list – otherwise you will be wasting your time.

Now look at the activities the trust is willing to fund. Often these will be stated in terms of restrictions – those activities that will not be considered. A trust that seemed appropriate up until this point might be ruled out if, for example, it doesn't fund events, and you are proposing a conference.

Now select your hit-list

Once you have your short-list you might need to do some further research to find out more about some of the trusts. The aim here is to pull out the ones with the most in common with your project, and put them at the top of your list.

If there is a published phone number in one of the directories then you could ring up to request any guidelines, if they exist. Some trust administrators will be willing to discuss your project over the phone. If there isn't a published phone number, this indicates the trust does not want to receive phone calls. You won't help your case by finding out the number by some other means and ringing up.

Once you have the additional information you need, then you should work through your short-list again to find the best matches between the trust's aims and what your project can achieve. The better the fit, the higher your chance of success. And the shorter your list, the more time and effort you can put into each application.

Who does the research?

The process we have described takes quite a large amount of time to do effectively. So who should actually do all this research?

You can do it yourself

You know your project in great depth, so it might be fairly easy for you to spot those trusts most likely to consider your application. You are probably the best person to carry out this task. However, you won't always have the time available. There are some other options.

Researcher/research agency

You might brief a researcher or research agency to come up with a hit-list on your behalf. However, this can be quite an expensive option for a small charity or community group, and the more research that is needed the higher the final cost. Any researcher will need to be thoroughly briefed, and they need fully to understand the case you have made for the project. You will need to be quite specific about the amount of detail you want on each trust, for the money you are paying the researcher.

The next step

Now that you have your hit-list of trusts, you will be ready to approach individual trusts with your proposal. You have already made the case for your project, in general terms, through your project proposal. Now you need to adapt this information to form an individually appropriate 'case for funding' for each trust on your hit-list.

Making your application

In this chapter we look at:

▶ How to present the case for your project in different and appropriate ways to different trusts
▶ How to complete application forms effectively
▶ What to submit in support of your proposal

Ready to apply?

You are ready to start making applications to grant-making trusts when you have:

- made the case for your project;
- all necessary supporting documents to hand;
- created a hit-list of trusts with aims that match your project;
- obtained any application forms required by trusts on your hit-list.

In this section we are going to look at how you can extract information from your project proposal – presenting this in application forms or proposals to different trusts.

Why have you chosen this trust?

You need to be clear about why you are making an application to this trust. What is it that you are trying to achieve?

As we have seen, it's not simply about asking someone to give you some money. It's about showing that you can help the trust to achieve its goals through your work and that therefore the trust should consider giving you a grant.

This is why sending a begging letter rarely works – the kind of letter in which a charity says 'we are desperately in need of support, please send us lots of money'. And it's why some trusts are put off by charities who think they have a right to funding – and say so.

Adapting your case

You have already prepared the case for your project. Now you need to adapt this for each trust on your hit-list.

For instance, you might use particular phrases that reflect the way a trust has stated its aims. You might ask for specific parts of your project to be funded by the trust because it is interested in a particular area, or because its grants are limited in size or duration.

Two options – a form or a proposal

Some trusts produce application forms. Most invite you to put the proposal to them in your own structure.

If a trust doesn't provide an application form, then it's completely up to you to decide which information to present and in what order – unless the trust has specifically said that you should send information under particular headings.

Completing application forms

Some of the larger trusts produce application forms. A form helps you to provide all the information the trust needs to complete a first assessment on your bid for funding. A form helps the trust to ensure it is consistent in its decision-making.

Many people struggle with forms; they are put off by the apparent bureaucracy. But it's important to see them as giving a structure to your application, and as something that will help a trust to assess your bid fairly.

You already have all the information you are likely to need to complete the form – it's laid out in your project proposal document and you should use this as your constant reference.

Different formats

Some trusts have application forms available to download from their website. This enables you to key the information in on your computer.

Other trusts supply the headings or questions for you to answer, but ask you to type up a proposal along these lines.

And some send out printed application forms. These need to be neatly hand-written, typed or fed through a printer (if they are the right size). It's always worth photocopying such forms and filling them in in draft, before using the top copy. If you have particular communication needs, then ask if the trust can make the information available to you in a suitable format.

Read the guidelines

If a trust issues an application form there will almost always be accompanying guidelines. These might be on the form itself or in a separate booklet.

You wouldn't apply for a job without reading the job description. Don't apply to a trust without reading its guidelines thoroughly!

The guidelines might say that some additional information must be attached. They could explain a complicated question in terms that are easier to understand. They might make it clear you aren't eligible for funding (so don't waste your time applying). They are there to help you and they should give you a better feel for the organisation you are approaching.

Answer the questions

Don't leave any questions on the form blank – even if you are attaching information. Summarise the essentials on the form before referring to attachments. The person reading the form needs to get a good idea of your project from the information included. This will then encourage them to read additional detail later.

Application forms are often used to filter out those proposals that the trust doesn't think fits its work, so that it can concentrate efforts on making choices from those that do. If you don't fill out the form properly you may lose this opportunity!

Answer all the questions carefully, checking that what you have written is what you mean. And don't make assumptions about which questions are more important than others. Try to answer all questions as well as possible.

If you find yourself repeating the same information in two different places, then you have probably misunderstood one of the questions. Application forms are designed to gather different bits of information, not to trick you by asking the same thing twice. So look again at the questions and any guidance notes.

Read back through your draft and ask whether this is all the information you would need to decide how well this project fits the trust's purpose. Then, as a final check, pass the draft to someone outside your organisation to see if they can easily understand and describe your project, based on the information you have provided. If they can, then you have done your organisation and your work justice. If they can't, then you might need to add to or amend the information.

Use phone calls appropriately

Some trusts will answer queries as you complete your application. This can be very useful but you should only contact a trust with a genuine enquiry. If the information you ask for is clearly in the guidelines which you haven't bothered to consult, then this may leave a bad impression of your organisation. On the other hand, don't be afraid to ask. It will help the trust to appreciate how its information is being used, and when anything is unclear. It can save both your organisation and the trust time too, if you answer questions appropriately in your initial application.

Completing your own proposal

Your individual proposal will work through the areas you have covered in the main project proposal. You should be able to use this document as the basis for each trust application, editing as appropriate. You have the freedom to decide on which pieces of information from the project proposal to use.

You should write a covering letter, and accompany this with the individually composed proposal, and supporting documentation. Below we are going to look at what you might include in these different elements.

The proposal

Your proposal should be concise and no more than four sides of A4 long if possible. You will probably also need to attach some supporting information, such as a copy of your latest annual report and accounts.

Keep the language clear and simple – avoid jargon wherever possible. It helps to keep sentences short and punchy. Your application should be enthusiastic, confident and logical.

Introduction

Your proposal should open with a clear statement of the need or problem you have identified, its relevance and importance, and how you plan to address this.

The project

Next you should state the aims, objectives and targets that you established when you made the case for your project.

Within this section of your proposal you can pick up on some of the areas you know to be of interest to the particular trust – using words and phrases you know will be meaningful to them.

Every application needs to be tailored for every trust.

A charity run by and for disabled people wanted to secure funding to develop a new training and job-seeking project. It approached a number of trusts successfully. But the terms in which it wrote to different organisations varied according to the trusts' particular interests/objects.

For example, one trust described its work in terms of providing support to disadvantaged groups. In writing to this organisation the charity outlined how its beneficiaries are disadvantaged within society and how the training and employment project helps to tackle this. In writing to another trust, which had a clear emphasis on development work by and for disabled people the charity talked in terms of user involvement and self-help. A third trust prioritised regeneration initiatives. The charity wrote describing the local unemployment rate, illiteracy levels, and the significant disadvantages faced by disabled people in the area of high deprivation.

After outlining aims, objectives and targets, you can describe the process – how you plan to deliver the project. Then you should explain how you plan to monitor the work. All of this information can be drawn from the case you made for your project. But again, the terminology and emphasis may differ in different applications.

Once you have provided an overview of the work you are planning, you should provide the evidence, or justification, for the project.

Justification

A trust will want to see evidence of need. You should be able to refer to the information you prepared in the main proposal for your project.

The Special Childcare Charity, for instance, said: 'at the moment the 250 children attending our daycare services have limited access to integrated facilities. They spend much of the time away from their families. According to a recent report from Central University, integrated learning and play environments offer a rich developmental experience for both disabled children and their siblings ... '

And the charity followed up this academic reference with something more personal ...

'We ran a pilot project last summer, following a suggestion from service users on our management committee. At the same time we conducted some family-based research work. This showed that 95 per cent of the children using our services, and their families, wanted to be involved in a full-scale integrated summer playscheme. Of these, 98 per cent said they felt it would be a beneficial experience for all who took part.'

Put some solid evidence behind your application. Convince the trust: it's not just that your organisation's fundraiser has had a bright idea – people want the project.

Costs and funding

You have already prepared your budget, so you can present this within your application.

You might provide it in full, or in a summarised form. And if you have some capital elements, explain how you will decide on the contractor.

At this point, you need to say clearly how much you are asking for. Again this will vary from trust to trust – and should fit within guidelines the trust provides on the sums of money it usually grants.

If you are looking for the full amount, you need to make this clear. If you are after a contribution, then you should say how much you want – not 'all contributions gratefully received', otherwise it smacks of a circular begging letter. As we said earlier, you should cost the project accurately and ask for a reasonable sum of money. Don't over- or under-cost any elements.

Ask for an amount that is within the trust's range of giving. If this isn't the full amount, you will need to say from where you expect to get the rest of your money. This might be a contribution from reserves, or community fundraising. It could be from sponsorship, the local council or other trusts, for example.

If you are approaching other trusts, you should say so to each one, and how much you have asked for. This will reassure the trust that if it makes a contribution you are likely to raise the balance. The trust might even ring round to find out how your requests have fared at the other trusts and foundations.

Your exit strategy

Finally, you should outline your exit strategy to show that you are already thinking about the sustainability of your project (or how it will continue after the initial funding has finished), and in what form that could be. This shows you have thought ahead and there is a clear developmental process. It may be that your project is planned to have a life of three years only. You must explain the rationale and who will learn from the experience.

Supporting information

If a trust is interested in your initial application, it might ask for further details. But you would usually include the following supporting information in any case. Make sure you include any extras that have been asked for in an application form.

Annual report and accounts

Most trusts expect you to enclose at least one set of annual reports and accounts. Some will ask for more.

If something unusual occurred in the last year, distorting your accounts, you might want to include some others from previous years with an explanation.

If your accounts show a large sum in your reserves, a trust will want to know why you are not spending this on your current project. If your accounts show a huge deficit, a trust will want to know what you are doing to address this, how you got into the situation, and the implications of how you might handle a grant from them. They want to make sure that the funding will be used for the project stated, not to plug the gap.

Constitution

Trusts fund charitable work. Many grant-making trusts and foundations only fund charities (some only registered charities).

If you are not a registered charity, or if you are a different kind of non-profit organisation, you should enclose a copy of your constitution (or set of rules). If you are a charity, then you should not send your constitution unless you are asked to supply it. If you do not have a constitution, then you should ask your CVS for advice.

Other supporting information

Trusts do not want to be weighed down with masses of paperwork or videos. So, you might be better off referring to additional information and saying that it is available on request. Some trusts might want, at a later stage, to see a detailed business plan. However, depending on your project and the trust concerned, you might want to attach details of any pilot work or research studies referred to in your application. A letter of endorsement or press cuttings might be appropriate. Some trusts actively discourage additional information at this stage; do read their guidelines carefully.

However, a letter from a beneficiary, a photo, or an illustration can really bring an application to life. They can capture the value of your whole organisation and its work, grabbing a trust's attention.

Further information

A trust might clearly state that it wants further documents. And these might include references, a job description (if you are applying for funding for a post), your equal opportunities policy and so on.

The trust might ask for this information with your initial application or after an initial read-through of your proposal – when you move on to the second stage of consideration.

A covering letter

You might want to make your whole proposal into a letter, in which case the points below illustrate how you can 'top and tail' your proposal. Alternatively, you might include a brief covering letter to summarise the key points covered in your application.

Introduce your organisation

You want the trust to know who is writing to it – and that means more than just your name. You need to give it a brief idea of the area of work in which you're involved and why you're writing.

> The Special Childcare Charity opened with:
>
> 'I am writing on behalf of The Special Childcare Charity – we provide early years care and development nursery facilities for disabled children.

> We are looking for funding for [or 'towards'] our summer playscheme for
> disabled children and their siblings ... '

From these opening sentences a trust will gather:

- who is asking for the funding;
- the essential aim of the project which needs funding.

A trust should be able to see from your opening statement that you are the sort of organisation it funds, and that you are asking for support for a project that relates to its funding themes.

You have already introduced your organisation with a brief sentence. You now need to explain more about the work you do. This information might include how long you have been in operation, and why the organisation was set up.

> The Special Childcare Charity explained:
>
> 'The Special Childcare Charity was set up 10 years ago by a group of
> parents of disabled children. The charity was established to provide a
> positive developmental environment for disabled children and their
> families. There was no such provision in the district ... '

In this paragraph you are explaining the work of your organisation and also demonstrating your credibility. You are showing how the particular project you want funded fits within your overall objects and work. It's worth including a reference to any accreditation, inspection (or quality control), significant achievements and so on in this section. This helps to show you are experienced and the right organisation to undertake such work.

So, the trust might think 'that's a worthwhile and well-run organisation. They know what they are doing. Now, why do they want to set up a summer playscheme?' (or whatever it was that you outlined in your opening statement). The important thing is that the trust should be excited by your project and want to read on.

At this stage you can pick up on the main headings within your proposal and briefly summarise:

- the project (a description and overall aim);
- the justification (a powerful piece of evidence of a problem or need);
- costs and funding (the overall cost and how much you are asking for).

Alternatively you can move into the full proposal at this stage, making the letter into one single proposal document.

Summarise your case

Why this trust? Your proposal should make a compelling case for the trust to fund your work. However, in your covering letter you can summarise why you have applied to this trust in particular – in a way helping it with its assessment of your application. Explain how your project will help fulfil its purpose.

> The Special Childcare Charity continued:
>
> 'We are applying to the Children's Foundation because:
>
> (a) you want to encourage improved access of disabled children to integrated services – our playscheme will achieve this for 250 young people;
>
> (b) you are looking to support family-based projects – our playscheme is designed to involve the whole family.'

An administrator could tell at a quick glance that your application fits the trust's overall guidelines (helping to achieve its purposes). The administrator will hopefully, therefore, put your application in the 'further consideration' pile, not in the bin.

Contact details

Whatever you do, don't forget to state your contact details, particularly if they are different from those on your main letterhead. Say when you are available – and give a contact number for normal office hours (when most trusts will want to get in touch). The trust might want to find out more about your application, so your best contact will be one who knows the project and whose enthusiasm will shine through. Not only should they know all about the project, but they should be clear about the overall work and direction of your organisation and its financial situation. If they don't know all the facts, they should know how to find out this information and feel confident talking about these issues.

It's worth thinking about the most appropriate person to sign off your letter (your chairperson, perhaps, if they are a well-known figure). Whoever signs your letter should be the person who is ready to take any queries resulting from the application.

And don't forget to use your organisation's letterhead, including your charity registration details as appropriate.

Correct addressee

Always find out to whom you should address the letter and where it should be sent. And use the appropriate ending – if you don't have a personal contact, then begin 'Dear Sir or Madam' and end with 'Yours faithfully'. It may seem obvious, but some people prepare standard letters and mail-merge them with addresses on their database. When they have some contact names, but not all, they often forget this point.

In fact, you shouldn't really be doing a mail-merge at all. Every letter should be specially written to each trust – with a reference to the trust's funding policies and the reason why you are approaching it. And if you are targeting just a dozen or so carefully selected trusts, then a mail-merge won't even save you time.

A final check

Before you send off your proposal or application form, check that you have:

- enclosed all the documentation requested;
- clearly addressed/highlighted all the areas of 'fit' between what your project can achieve and the interests of the trust.

Now is the moment to ask someone who knows nothing about the project and application to read it. Can they summarise what it is you are asking for? Are they convinced?

Keep a copy of everything

Before sealing the envelope on your application, take a copy of all the paperwork. Then file it within easy reach, so that if you receive a call asking for further information you can refer to it effortlessly.

What happens next?

Once you have put a significant effort into researching and writing your trust applications it can feel quite an achievement. What, though, happens next?

In some cases the answer might sadly be 'nothing'. You might never hear back from some trusts. However, most trusts will come back to you, even if it is to say 'no'.

You might hear nothing for quite some time. But you will be more likely to get a positive response if you have prepared your proposals carefully and have been very selective in who you have approached.

In the next chapter we look at the different stages your proposal will go through as it is assessed by the various trusts.

Assessment

In this chapter you will find out about:

▸ What a trust is looking for in the applications it receives
▸ What happens when a trust assesses your application
▸ Common stumbling blocks that may lead to applications being turned down
▸ How soon you might hear and what you might be told by a trust

What is a trust looking for?

Trusts are looking for projects that help them achieve their purpose. They are looking for projects that meet their funding policies, priorities or criteria.

These projects are likely to be run by organisations that:

- have a charitable purpose;
- are financially sound;
- are not trying to replace state funding of their project;
- have the management capacity to run the project;
- have an achievable project plan, including a sensible budget.

Remember that the person assessing your application has to be able to put forward a convincing argument in favour of funding your project to the trustees. This person needs to make a case for funding (just as you did originally) and all they have to go on is the information you have provided, and possibly some other supporting information from a third party or other source.

The process of filtering applications

People looking at applications consciously or unconsciously take the application through a filtering system which might look like this:

First filter

- Does it fit our purpose?
- Is it generally within all policies and priorities?
- Can we afford it?

Second filter

- How and why does it fit our purpose? And how well does it fit?
- Does it fit our other funding policies?
- Can this organisation do it? How well?
- Can we afford to commit this sum to this project?
- How much are we justified in committing?
- Can they make this project happen, and when?

Trusts are always looking for evidence – facts with substantive arguments, rather than a gut feel.

However, there is a human element that's worth remembering. The person in your organisation who has developed the project, and who will be running it, will probably feel passionately about the need for the project. If a trust talks to this person, their enthusiasm and commitment can have a powerful effect on the outcome of your application.

Trusts know that many projects succeed because of committed individuals within voluntary groups.

But there is a downside to this which the trust must consider. And that is the question of what happens if that committed individual leaves the organisation – will the project come to an end?

What is assessment?

It's worth considering what assessment is all about. It is not a test! Whether a trust talks to you on the phone or visits you, this is a genuine attempt to find out more about you and your project.

- Assessment is a process which helps the trust to determine how well the application fits with its purpose, and falls within its policies, priorities and criteria.
- It is a way of ensuring that what you've written has been properly understood.
- It is an information-gathering exercise which enables the assessor to write a report in 'trust speak' for their own trustees.
- It is an opportunity to make sure that applicants are treated fairly – sometimes the written word doesn't do the project justice.
- It enables trustees to make informed choices about which applications they want to fund.

What would you fund and why?

What would it be like for you to be in the shoes of a trustee? How would you make the decisions on what to fund? Thinking about this will help you to appreciate why a trust might ask you particular questions and how best to present your organisation and project.

What would your organisation fund if you suddenly had a large sum of money to distribute?

Think about the size of grant you might award, the geographical area you would cover, the focus or themes for funding and so on. It helps you to appreciate the work involved and the dilemmas faced by trusts when they make their grants.

The trust's perspective

It can be helpful to consider things from the trust's perspective. A trust wants to give its money to support good quality work within its chosen area. Over time it will build up an idea of how many applications it can expect to receive each day or week, and how many, on average, it will be able to fund.

Trusts are working with limited sums of money. At times they may have to turn down good applications because they simply don't have enough money to go round.

In some cases trusts say 'yes' to all applications they want to support, and operate a kind of queuing system – when funds become available they are paid to the next charity in line. Others have funding rounds with deadlines and a set sum of money to allocate.

Some trusts say 'yes' to appropriate applications until they have used up their budget. Others make monthly decisions, with a set sum of money allocated.

Trusts want to be excited and inspired by the letters they receive. They are not, generally, trying to catch you out or find reasons for turning you down. They are more likely to be looking for reasons to support you.

When a trust receives your application one of the first things it will consider is who the request comes from.

If the trust doesn't know you

If a trust hasn't heard of your organisation before, it will want to know what you do, whether you are uniquely meeting a particular need, the geographical area you service, where you are based, and how well regarded you are in your field (amongst other things.)

You can answer most of these points on your application form or in your proposal. The final one is more difficult. Other people can say you are wonderful, but it doesn't sound so convincing if you say it yourself.

You might be able to help by including endorsements or press cuttings. Some trusts will want to meet you and your organisation to find out for themselves.

The assessment of your application

Each trust has its own particular approach to assessing applications. In many cases the trustees will consider almost all applications at regular meetings.

The larger trusts, with administrators, might delegate the authority to screen out obviously inappropriate submissions. And the biggest employ trained grant officers or administrators to carry out initial assessments and make recommendations.

The decision on whether or not to fund a project always remains ultimately with the trustees.

Scrutinising your information

At the very least the appropriate people within the trust will read your application thoroughly – considering some or all of the issues outlined above. And they will probably compare (from their experience) your application with others before concluding that they should, or should not, consider supporting you.

Asking for further details

Many trusts will ask you for further information on a particular aspect of your proposal. This shows that they are taking your application seriously – it hasn't been ruled out at the first hurdle. However, this is by no means a guarantee that you will be successful.

Telephone interviews

Some trusts carry out telephone interviews with applicants who are through the initial stage of assessment. Don't feel under pressure to respond there and then. Agree to speak at a time when you can concentrate on the call. Ask what they want to cover, and get the information together – read it before the interview. Ask how long they think the call will last. And at the end of the call, remember to forward any information you have promised to send.

Visits

A few trusts make visits to applicants before making their decision. Visits can be nerve-racking. But they are an opportunity. They may be a sign that you are near to receiving a grant, but again they are not a guarantee. Meetings are a chance to explain your project in great detail. And they are ideal for showing what a difference the trust's funding could make.

The important thing is to be well-prepared, showing practical work in action. A site visit shouldn't involve a couple of people in suits sitting in the charity's office – that isn't the best way to show the commitment and enthusiasm of beneficiaries, staff and volunteers.

If a trust wants to arrange a visit, always ask what they want to see, along with:

- the range of questions they want to cover;
- who they want to talk to;
- if they want to pursue financial matters (you may need your treasurer on hand).

Independent views

Some trusts ask for independent views from experts in your field of work, or on particular aspects of a project (e.g. an architect if you are working on a major capital project).

The need for confidence

Your application might sound fantastic on paper. But this isn't enough. A trust needs to believe in you, and have confidence in your ability to do the work effectively.

Trusts are willing to take risks

Having said all that, there are trusts which are willing to take risks. They will, on occasion, back new organisations with interesting yet untested ideas. But they still need to believe that the project will succeed.

How can you fill a trust with confidence?

Some of the things that will fill a trust with confidence are:

- the personnel involved – their abilities, past achievements and commitment;
- strong evidence of need – good research into what is needed and wanted, and full user involvement;

- well thought-through plans – with contingency measures and evidence that you are already thinking about what happens when the funding comes to an end;
- independent expert support for the idea.

Common stumbling blocks

Even though a trust isn't looking to trip you up, they will consider some of the following points.

- **Funding problems at organisational level** – a large deficit accrued over time suggests poor financial management. Equally, massive reserves need a good strategic explanation if they are to be accepted. Trusts certainly won't give a grant if you can't demonstrate financial need or financial capability.
- **Constitutional difficulties** – if a group doesn't have a constitution or a set of rules, or there's commercial gain involved, then the application won't get any further consideration.
- **Lack of cost effectiveness** – if administrative costs are very high and the overall cost of the service more than one would expect, or if the project only provides low levels of benefit for the amount it costs, then it won't be funded.
- **Controversy** – if a project is political, overtly campaigning, not wanted locally, or in some other way controversial it might prove impossible for a trust to fund.
- **Lack of user consultation** – if there is no evidence of user consultation or need, then it will appear that the project is being imposed. The trust will be looking for user endorsement and involvement.
- **Large grant/small organisation** – organisations take, and need, time to grow. A massive injection of cash can unbalance an organisation, and the project may never have the opportunity to flourish. This can raise many more problems later on, particularly in terms of what happens when the funding ends.

Approval processes and feedback

At the end of all this deliberation, the trustees will decide on whether to give you a grant or not.

The decision on whether or not to accept your application for funding is always taken at a trustees' meeting. These meetings generally have packed agendas. Often there is a pile of applications for consideration, and the trustees work through them until the time runs out. They might consider all of them. Some requests are carried over to the next meeting. This is fine if the trustees meet each month. It's more disappointing if they meet just once a quarter or less. Things can be considerably delayed.

No response

Some trusts say that they will make contact only with successful applicants. This saves on the cost of administration, but it's frustrating for the applicant who doesn't know if they have been considered yet.

Stamped addressed postcard

Other trusts will send an acknowledgement or turn you down by returning a stamped addressed postcard. At least you know the answer, even if it's disappointing.

Refusal and no explanation

It feels slightly better to receive a personalised letter turning you down. But it's not very enlightening if there is no explanation as to why you weren't successful. You don't know if it's worth applying again in the future for similar projects.

If you are turned down without any explanation, you might want to ask why. However, you are only likely to get feedback from trusts who have administrative staff or well-publicised grants programmes. Remember, the staff don't make decisions. If an answer is available, asking questions about why you have been turned down can only ever put you in a better position to re-apply.

Refusal and feedback

Some trusts do provide an explanation of why you have been turned down. Sometimes this is offered by phone – and is quite specific. In other cases, there is a letter with more general details.

A formal grant offer

When your application is successful you will be made a grant offer. Some trusts will send you a grant offer and cheque at the same time! You might be rung first, but you will always receive an offer in writing. This might be for all that you asked for, part of what you asked for or (rarely) more than you asked for.

The grant offer will usually come with terms and conditions – outlining what the money is for, on what basis the grant will be paid over, and the funding timetable. The grant may be paid in instalments, or in a lump sum. Some trusts will also tell you about their monitoring requirements. If they don't, then ask. It's easier to make sure you will be able to provide the details they need in 12 months time if you know what that is now. It won't send you into a frantic search for facts and figures later.

The information required will usually be much the same as the information you require to run the project effectively, and make judgements about how well you are achieving the project's aims and objectives.

Working with trusts

In this chapter we look at:

▶ How you can develop and nurture your relationship with a trust
▶ The way different trusts attach terms and conditions to their funding
▶ How trusts might make their payments to you
▶ The need to monitor and evaluate your work

Once a trust has agreed to your request for funding this is the beginning, not the end. It's worth celebrating your success – all your efforts have paid off and your valuable work has been recognised. And it might be helpful to reflect on why you have succeeded – in case there are lessons to learn for the future.

Fundraising is a means to an end. Now it's time to get on with the project, and to build an effective relationship with your trust funders. This relationship may be guided by the terms and conditions under which you are offered a grant.

Terms and conditions

Details of any terms and conditions will usually be included with the grant offer letter. You might be asked to read through these and send a confirmation that you accept the terms and would like to accept the grant.

If you don't understand them or they seem difficult, talk to the trust before signing.

Some trusts will simply send you a cheque and wish you well.

Whether or not the trust requires you to report back on how you spent the grant, it is a matter of courtesy to let it know what happened. Saying 'thank you' may be the trigger for it to consider a further application from your organisation.

When and how the money will be paid

Trusts usually pay by one of the following methods.

- **Payment by cheque** – most trusts will send you a cheque (or cheques).
- **Directly into a bank account** – some trusts make payments directly into your bank account. To do this they will need your account details.

- **Staged payments** – in some cases, particularly with larger grants, the money will be paid in stages. The amounts might be split to reflect your spending projections, especially if the funding is annual over three years. In other cases there might be tapering payments (these get smaller with each payment). Tapered payments can reflect the trust's gradual withdrawal from the project.
- **Advance versus retrospective** – trusts usually have thousands of pounds at their disposal. It is obviously unfair to expect a small charity to cash-flow a project, so most trusts will be sympathetic to a request for money in advance of the work being done.

Accounting for the money

You will be expected to show how you have spent the money. And this could include the production of copies of invoices or receipts for payments, bank statements and your end-of-year accounts.

It is reasonable for a trust to want to ensure that the money it has given has been used appropriately. Check on reporting arrangements before you start spending.

As well as checking how the money has been spent, the trust may well want to monitor your organisation's performance, or work. In addition, the trust might want an evaluation of the project's impact. We return to these issues in more detail below.

Termination

The terms and conditions will normally outline any circumstances under which your grant could be withdrawn. This protects the trust against you using the money inappropriately. And the money might have to be repaid in full, if this is in the terms of your grant.

Other terms and conditions

There may be other terms and conditions depending on the nature of your project and the particular funder. These might include arrangements to publicise and disseminate the findings of your project; recruitment and employment conditions; and other specific policies.

Keeping your end of the bargain

The terms and conditions of your grant should be a reminder that you need to carry out the work outlined in your application. You expect the trust to pay over the promised money at the time it has specified. So, the trust can reasonably expect you to do all you said in your original proposal. This is why it is so important to be realistic and truthful in this proposal, without 'overclaiming.'

Delivering on your promises

Your project plan, prepared before your application, will be essential in helping you to deliver your promises. Your plan should include a detailed timetable and outline of actions needed.

If you think there is a problem at any stage, then it is essential to discuss it openly with your trust funder. The trust is likely to be more sympathetic if it is involved at an early stage. It might know of similar difficulties encountered by other organisations it funds – and suggest a solution. It might be willing to adapt its agreement or funding levels to reflect the problem.

We have already said that some trusts are prepared to be flexible and to take risks. Many will be prepared to work with you to help try to solve any problem. They, like you, want your project to succeed.

And many will acknowledge that the best laid plans may have to change if the project's purpose is to be achieved. Plans change because circumstances change. Some you have control over, others you don't.

Approaches to monitoring and evaluation

Just as trusts differ enormously over funding criteria, they have contrasting approaches to monitoring and evaluation.

Monitoring involves checking on performance: Have you done what you said you would do at the appropriate time? How many people have used your service? It is about being accountable.

Evaluation explores the impact and value of your work: What have you achieved? Has it been worthwhile? This usually takes place at the end of the project.

Monitoring can, to a large extent, involve regular reports from the grant recipient to the trust. The trust might want to make some sort of independent check on these claims.

Evaluation can also be carried out by the organisation itself. But sometimes an independent review is needed.

Of course, the level of monitoring and evaluation should reflect the size of the grant. A small grant of £250, for example, could hardly justify an independent evaluation of what's been achieved. Even asking the grant recipient to prepare their own analysis of the effect of a grant of £250 would be an unnecessary burden.

Monitoring reports and visits

You might be asked to produce regular reports to enable the trust to monitor your progress. The trust itself might complete these reports, ringing you up for the information required.

Some trusts conduct monitoring visits. The visits might be used to gather information for a report. Or they might be a double-check on what you have told the trust.

If you have to prepare a regular report you should agree the format and content with the trust. Then you can adapt and update it as needed. The danger is always to want to impress the trust and then to spend too long and give too much information – making a simple task over-complicated and stressful.

Internal evaluation

You might be asked to evaluate the impact of the project. This will usually mean producing one final report, but there might be an interim or annual report if funding is over a couple of years.

Evaluation starts with the purpose, or aims, of the project. You want to demonstrate the changes that have taken place because of what you have done, and the difference this has made to the people involved.

Always leave room for unexpected outcomes. You might find that you have achieved quite a bit more than you set out to, or that there have been spin-off benefits that you did not anticipate. You might discover another unmet need that could be the beginning of another project.

External evaluation

Only a few trusts pay for projects to be evaluated independently. This is appropriate for some of the larger-scale projects. Someone from the outside is often able to bring a fresh eye to your work, and may make valuable suggestions as to how it can be developed and improved.

How should you involve trust funders in your work?

Your trust funder will tell you the terms under which it is giving you the grant, possibly saying how it wants to be kept informed. However, your relationship doesn't have to be one of powerful funder and terribly grateful recipient charity. It can be much more balanced, more of a partnership.

Appropriate levels of involvement

You are one half of the relationship with a trust. You might want to have a creative partnership with them. However, some want to operate at arm's length. There's nothing you can do in this situation, apart from keeping them informed and being open and friendly with them.

Other trusts will be more willing to hear from you, to discuss progress and plans, and even suggest future funding opportunities.

Some of the larger trusts like to be more actively involved in projects. They might meet as part of a steering committee. They might like to come along to different events, or simply visit to see your work in action.

No one trust has the same approach. And individual trustees and administrators have their own preferred way of working. So, you can't rush their active involvement; instead you have to respond to the particular organisation and individual.

Saying 'thank you'

Even if you are dealing with a very distant trust, you should always say 'thank you' when you receive an offer of funding, and when the money itself arrives.

Your letter should, of course, be enthusiastic and positive and refer to what you plan to do. This is polite, it will show the trust how much you value its support, and will leave a good impression. It doesn't take long to write such a letter.

Keeping trusts informed

As well as sending trusts formal reports on progress, it is good to keep them up-to-date with other information. This might be your regular newsletter, with fairly general details of your organisation, or it might be literature connected with the project itself.

If a trust is happy for you to ring with information or questions, then this is a good way of building a personal relationship. At the same time, sending written information, or samples of leaflets and so on, gives the trust something tangible for its files.

Publicity

We have already seen that some trusts like to keep a low profile. Many, though, are keen on publicity – for the project they are supporting, but not for themselves as this is likely to generate demand for funding when they are already oversubscribed.

Publicising the grant awarded

If a trust is publicity shy, issuing a press release could get your relationship off to a bad start. You will therefore need to work together with such a trust if you intend to announce details of your award.

The press release will say who has received the grant, for how much, and from whom. Then, possibly, it will give a bit of context about the grant – saying how many others have been awarded locally, or under which particular programme of grants it has been made. The release will go on to elaborate on the project, and who will benefit, before including an enthusiastic quote from the grant recipient.

Finally, further information on the grant recipient and the trust should close the press release, as in the example opposite.

In this example the main focus of the press release is on what the charity will be able to do, thanks to the generous funding it has received. That is what will interest the general public who read the papers. Even if the sum awarded was £5 million, the main issues are 'Why is it needed?' and 'What will it be used for?'

As well as explaining about the grant, the press release is an opportunity to say a bit more about the general work and aims of the group. Who knows, another trust reading the report just might think: 'Well, the Big Foundation thinks they are worth supporting, and we're funding self-build projects ... perhaps they'd be interested in applying to us.'

Keep any cuttings!

Special thank you events

One final way of saying thank you, and building a relationship with your funder, is to hold one or more special events. These shouldn't be lavish, costly affairs (or the trust may wonder why you need its money). Thank you events can be simple open days, where you show off your work and at the same time publicly thank your funders.

Such events can make a lasting impression. And they can be a good occasion on which to discuss your future plans.

'Perhaps the trust might like to support this next big idea ...'

Example press release

issued: 4 June

subject: Big Foundation grant 1 of 1

Housing Charity Receives £50,000 Cash Boost from the Big Foundation

Housing charity, Youth Action on Homelessness, will open a new centre in Gainshire, thanks to a grant of £50,000 from the Big Foundation.

The money has been awarded as part of the foundation's Young People At Risk programme.

The new centre will open next year and will offer support and advice to young people who are thinking of leaving home, or who are homeless.

Youth Action on Homelessness director, Jane Frost, said: 'We are delighted to have been awarded such a large grant. The money means we can expand our work and help over 500 additional young people each year. Homelessness and housing problems make young people particularly vulnerable. Our centre will advise them on low-cost rented accommodation, training and employment opportunities, and benefit entitlements. We will also be working with local health and welfare agencies.'

YAH has been operating since 1987. It hopes to set up a self-build initiative where young people build their own homes, whilst receiving valuable training.

The Big Foundation provides grants of up to £100,000 to charities working with young people at risk.

For further information contact: Jane Frost on 0X0 000

[ends]

Further information

In this section we outline details of some of the helpful organisations, publications and sources of advice mentioned throughout this guide.

Organisations

Association of Charitable Foundations (ACF)
2 Plough Yard
Shoreditch High Street
London EC2A 3LP
Tel 020 7422 8600
Fax 020 7422 8606
The UK-wide body representing trusts and foundations. ACF runs seminars and conferences for its members, helps to develop good practice guides, and encourages the exchange of information and advice between hundreds of trusts and foundations.

Charities Aid Foundation (CAF)
Kings Hill
West Malling
Kent ME19 4TA
Tel 01732 520000
www.cafonline.org (for news and case studies)
www.ngobooks.org.uk (to order books)
The Charities Aid Foundation provides financial services to charities and donors, including the Give As You Earn payroll giving scheme. Books previously published by CAF are now available through the Directory of Social Change.

Charity Commission
Harmsworth House
13–15 Bouverie Street
London EC4Y 8DP
Tel 0870 333 0123

Community Foundations Network
2 Plough Yard
Shoreditch High Street
London EC2A 3LP
Tel 020 7422 8611

The Directory of Social Change (DSC)
24 Stephenson Way
London NW1 2DP
Liverpool office:
Federation House
Hope Street
Liverpool L1 9BW
Publications and subscriptions:
Tel 020 7209 5151
Fax 020 7209 5049
Marketing and research:
(London) Tel 020 7209 4422
(Liverpool) Tel 0151 708 0136
Courses and conferences:
(London) Tel 020 7209 4949
(Liverpool) 0151 708 0117
Charityfair:
Tel 020 7209 4949
or 020 7209 1015 (exhibitors)
DSC is a registered charity set up to help voluntary organisations become more effective. It provides information and training and organises Charityfair, the biggest annual forum for the sector.

European Foundation Centre
rue de la Concorde 51,
B-1050 Bruxelles
Belgium
Tel (+32) 2 512 8938

Federation of Charity Advice Services (FCAS)
11 Upper York Street
Wakefield WF1 3LQ
Tel 01924 239063
This organisation represents charity information bureaux, charity advice services and others supporting voluntary groups in search of funding.

Institute of Charity Fundraising Managers (ICFM)
1 Nine Elms Lane
London SW8 5NQ
Tel 020 7627 3436
Fax 020 7627 3508
ICFM produces good practice guides, and represents fundraisers for the voluntary sector. It runs training sessions on a wide variety of fundraising matters, and holds an annual conference.

National Association of Councils for Voluntary Service (NACVS)
3rd Floor
Arundel Court
177 Arundel Street
Sheffield S1 2NU
Tel 0114 278 6636
NACVS is the national body for councils of voluntary service. It produces a directory of these local development organisations.

National Association of Volunteer Bureaux (NAVB)
New Oxford House
16 Waterloo Street

Birmingham B2 5UG
Tel 0121 633 4555
NAVB is the national body representing volunteer bureaux. It provides help and advice, and publishes a directory.

National Council for Voluntary Organisations (NCVO)
Regent's Wharf
8 All Saints Street
London N1 9RL
Tel 020 7713 6161

National Lottery Charities Board (NLCB)
For application forms for the main grants programmes:
Tel 08457 919191
For application forms for Awards for All:
Tel 0845 6002040
www.nlcb.org.uk
For the grant assessment manual website:
www.nlcb.org.uk/english/general/gam
NLCB is one of the distributors of lottery funding. Although not a trust, NLCB acts in much the same way as a trust or foundation and is a member of ACF. NLCB has had a major impact on both grant-making trusts and foundations, and the charities and community groups seeking support.

Retired Executives Action Clearing House (REACH)
Bear Wharf
27 Bankside
London SE1 9ET
Tel 020 7928 0452

**Retired Senior Volunteer
Programme (RSVP)**
237 Pentonville Road
London N1 9NJ
Tel 020 7278 6601

Publications

All titles in this list are available from DSC (see contact details in *Organisations* above). Phone 020 7209 5151 for a free publications list. Prices were correct at time of going to press but may be subject to change.

Trusts guides

CD-ROM Trusts Guide
2nd edition, DSC, 1999, £129.25 (inc. VAT)
Contains all the data from the Guides to Major Trusts Vols. 1 and 2 *and all* four Guides to Local Trusts.

Dimensions 2000
Volume 3 – Patterns of Independent Grant making in the UK
15th edition, CAF, 2000, £25.00
This special report presents the results of the first UK survey of independent trust and foundation funding distribution in the UK and includes analysis of and insights into, among others, priority subject areas, beneficiary groups and geographical areas funded.

The Directory of Grant Making Trusts 1999-2000 (DGMT)
16th edition, CAF, 1999, £89.95 (3 vols)
Volume 1 contains indexes by geographical area, field of interest, type of beneficiary and type of grant. Volume 2 is the main register, listing trusts in alphabetical order. Volume 3 gives detailed commentaries on 250 major trusts. The DGMT is based largely on information provided to the compilers of the directory by trusts themselves.

Grantseeker CD-ROM 2000
Release 3, Feb. 2000, £58.69
An interactive CD-ROM version of the DGMT. From 2001 Grantseeker *will be amalgamated with DSC's CD-ROM* Trusts Guide *to produce one comprehensive database for researchers.*

A Guide to the Local Trusts in Greater London
Sarah Harland, 2nd edition, DSC, 1999, £17.95

A Guide to the Local Trusts in the Midlands
Louise Walker, 2nd edition, DSC, 1999, £17.95

A Guide to the Local Trusts in the North of England
Louise Walker, 2nd edition, DSC, 1999, £17.95

A Guide to the Local Trusts in the South of England
Sarah Harland, 2nd edition, DSC, 1999, £17.95
These guides provide specific information on trusts which focus their grant making on particular geographical areas.

A Guide to the Major Trusts Vol. 1
Luke FitzHerbert, Dominic Addison and Faisel Rahman, 7th edition, DSC, 1999, £19.95

A Guide to the Major Trusts Vol. 2
Dave Casson and Sarah Harland, 4th
edition, DSC, 2000, £19.95

A Guide to the Major Trusts Vol. 3
Sarah Harland and Louise Walker, 1st
edition, DSC, 2000, £17.95
*These guides give a critical analysis of
the grant making of the UK's top trusts
and foundations. Volume 1 contains
the top 300 trusts; Volume 2 covers a
further 700; Volume 3 outlines another
400 UK-wide trusts, with further
details on major trusts in Northern
Ireland, Scotland and Wales.*

**Guide to the National Lottery
Charities Board**
Luke FitzHerbert, DSC, 2000, £15.00
*This independent guide gives
comprehensive details of the activities
of the National Lottery Charities
Board (NLCB). It includes an
annotated version of the NLCB's grant
assessment manual.*

The Guide to UK Company Giving
John Smyth, 3rd edition, DSC, 2000,
£25.00
*The essential reference for anyone
seeking to raise money or win support
from companies. Also available on CD-
ROM.*

Trust Monitor
Editor: Susan Forrester
Subscription £30.00 per year (£80.00
for three years)
*Published by DSC three times a year,
this magazine provides useful news
and information on developments in
the world of trusts and foundations.*

Specialist funding guides

The Arts Funding Guide
Susan Forrester and Graeme Manuel,
5th edition, DSC, 2000, £12.95

The Environmental Funding Guide
Susan Forrester and Dave Casson, 3rd
edition, DSC, 1998, £16.95

South Asian Funding in the UK
Karina Holly and Zerbanoo Gifford,
1st edition, DSC, 1999, £9.95

The Sports Funding Guide
Nicola Eastwood, 2nd edition, DSC,
1999, £16.95

The Youth Funding Guide
Nicola Eastwood, 1st edition, DSC,
1997, £15.95

Fundraising handbooks

Avoiding the Wastepaper Basket
Tim Cook, 2nd edition, LVSC, 1998,
£5.50

Find the Funds
A New Approach to Fundraising
Research
Christopher Carnie, DSC, 2000, £12.95
*This book answers the key question
that all fundraisers ask: 'Where is the
money?', with a section on funding
from trusts.*

Trust Fundraising
Ed. Anthony Clay, 1st edition,
CAF/ICFM, 1999, £19.95

**Writing Better Fundraising
Applications**
Michael Norton and Mike Eastwood,
2nd edition, DSC, 1997, £12.95

Appendix: Top Trusts

The information in this section is taken from the *Guides to the Major Trusts* and *Guides to the Local Trusts* (1999/2000 editions) published by DSC. For the local trusts, the grant total represents the amount, or an estimated amount, given in the relevant local area.

The top 20 trusts ranked by grant total

Grants	Trust	Main grant areas
£320,000,000	National Lottery Charities Board	Those at greatest disadvantage in society
£227,000,000	Wellcome Trust	Biomedical research, history of medicine, public understanding of science
£39,000,000	Foundation for Sport and the Arts	Sport, the arts
£28,591,000	Gatsby Charitable Foundation	Technical education, mental/other health, economic and social research, children/young people, welfare, development in Africa, plant sciences, arts, general
£22,717,000	Tudor Trust	Social welfare, general
£22,430,000	Garfield Weston Foundation	Arts, education, health, general
£21,000,000	Henry Smith Charity (Kensington Estate)	Social welfare, disability, health, medical research
£18,336,000	Wolfson Foundation	Hospitals and university medical departments, health
£17,711,000	BBC Children in Need Appeal	Child welfare
£17,000,000	PPP Healthcare Medical Trust	Healthcare
£15,240,000	Leverhulme Trust	Research and education
£12,821,000	Linbury Trust	Major capital projects, chronic fatigue syndrome, arts/art education, drug abuse, education
£11,654,000	Northern Ireland Voluntary Trust	Social welfare
£11,589,000	Esmée Fairbairn Charitable Trust	Social welfare, arts and heritage, education, environment, social and economic research

£10,100,000	Bridge House Estates Trust Fund	Welfare in London
£10,000,000	Help the Aged	Day centres, hospices, general, for the elderly
£9,036,000	Lloyds TSB Foundation for England and Wales	Social and community needs, education and training
£8,000,000	Northern Rock Foundation	People with disabilities and their carers
£7,530,000	Rank Foundation	Christian communication, youth, education, general
£6,770,000	Rowntree Foundation	Research and development in social policy

The top local trusts
Northern Ireland

Grants	Trust	Main grant areas
£11,654,000	Northern Ireland Voluntary Trust	Social welfare
£5,100,000	Ireland Funds	Peace and reconciliation, culture, community, education
£1,529,000	BBC Children in Need Appeal, NI	Disadvantaged children
£1,100,000	Lloyds TSB Foundation in Northern Ireland	Social and community needs, education and training, scientific and medical research
£124,000	Enkalon Foundation	Community, self-help, unemployed, welfare
£100,000	Ultach Trust	Irish language activities
£100,000	Esmé Mitchell Trust	Heritage, arts and culture
£81,000	John Moores Foundation	Social welfare
£77,000	Women Caring Trust	Children and families
£71,000	Lawlor Foundation	Social welfare, education, general